WARNING:

You should NOT purchase this playbook if you are not serious about taking on a radically different (but extremely effective) system to land a better job or career. If your preference is to continue doing the same old thing (resumes, want ads, electronic job postings) as part of the job search process then this book is not appropriate for you.

This is not written to insult you but rather to make sure you know that when you purchase this playbook and follow its 6 week program to get you up and running and engaged actively with multiple companies' hiring managers, to obtain optimal results you will be required to WORK HARD AND SMART!!

This playbook was created, written and organized with the sole purpose of being a real guide and help for serious job finding and acquisition. Use it in the same way that coaches use their playbooks. They refer to it constantly but they also modify it as conditions and new offense/defense strategies present themselves. Much thought was invested in such things as:

- how it is designed – so you can write in it and dog ear it but the main point here is to USE it!
- how it is structured - following a 6 week (kick you in the butt) program.
- the size of the book - 8.5 x 11 inches with note space provided on each page for writing and note-taking or those "ah hah" moments that need to be written down
- the examples and anecdotes – to provide real-life perspective and encouragement
- the perspectives from the other side of the hiring desk – to give you a do's and don'ts
- the methodology laid out in easily understandable steps - so you don't lose time and waste efforts

This playbook outlines a dramatically different process for pursuing the job/career of your desire but requires you to suspend possible doubt and skepticism. Why? Because this book's methods run counter to what the conventional wisdom of job getting have taught us!

What was the inspiration for this system? It came about when, at the age of 40, I found myself unemployed and looking for a job. I had recently moved from Seattle to Washington DC (a totally new market) with no personal connections and was looking to change industries (from logistics to security) while also seeking a 20% pay increase to cover the cost of living difference. Could I have stacked the deck against myself any higher? Were the requirements I needed to hit any harder? Yet I was able to achieve all the metrics above and so have others by following the steps outlined in this playbook.

Still interested? Then please read on!

John Lee

Copyright © 2013 LeeCore

Publisher: LeeCore Publishing

Cover design by Sandra Owen Design

"…, be ye therefore wise as serpents, and harmless as doves."
Matthew 10:16b (KJV)

This book is dedicated to:

Jesus, my Lord, who is my ultimate Inspiration and allowed a re-set of my life!

My sweet wife Sandy who has been my hard working muse

My precious two boys, Preston and Ellis who are reminders of why I do what I do

Darren, my nephew, who took the challenge and won

AND

To all those who struggle to improve their lives and their family's lives… **there is a better way!**

Further Acknowledgements:

I thank Sandy Owen for her great formatting and design work throughout this endeavor!

I thank Robert Baggats, Kappie Bogart, Katie Kay, Nathan Long and Elise Touchette for their help smoothing out the flow and adding more verve!

Contents

Chapter 1
The Psychology of Unemployment **9**

Chapter 2
What Doesn't Work (Anymore) **12**

Chapter 3
Desperation = Inspiration **21**

Chapter 4
Template for What Really Works. **26**

Chapter 5
Darren's Story. **30**

Chapter 6
A Fresh New Start **33**

Chapter 7
Week 1 - Preparation. **35**

Chapter 8
Week 2 - Research Industries and Topics **39**

Chapter 9
Week 3 - Research Topics **44**

Chapter 10
Week 4 - Engaging Targets. **48**

Chapter 11
Week 5 - Multiple Targets Engaged **55**

Chapter 12
Week 6 - Interviewing Process. **60**

Chapter 13
Look Back **67**

Chapter 14
Look Forward. **70**

Exhibits **71**

CHAPTER 1
The Psychology of Unemployment

The Thump When You Hit the Curb

When people become unemployed it is a very jarring event regardless of whether it is the first time or if they have gone down this road many times before. The mind always flits to the worst parts, which are:

- How much time and money will I need to invest/spend before I get my next job?
- How is this going to affect my ability to pay my bills?
- What are short term things I have to do to shift priorities?
- How will this look on my resume?
- How can I spin this to look good or at least acceptable to employers?

PRO NOTES:

For people who are in their 50' and 60's, there is another challenge – that of age, salary/benefits, and skills. When you get kicked to the curb at this age range, you feel like the baby chick that fell out of the warm, safe nest. The questions of your marketability and how you stack up to the younger workers in such a ruggedly demanding business market comes into the forefront of your mind. Sorry to say but it is also on the hiring manager's mind as well.

But the most daunting and painful realization is: I have to go through this crap all over again...networking, interviewing, job fairs, want ads, updating cover letters and resumes, blah blah blah? Ugh!!!

The situation is made even worse when the economy is in the tank! With huge numbers of people that are smart, sharp professionals recently off-loaded onto the unemployment rolls, it further decreases the chances of anyone getting a job much less a job/career you might desire.

Most of us feel that we can demonstrate that we can do the jobs we apply for IF we can just get in front of the hiring manager(s) but the challenge is to get that opportunity. The problem is that you have to overcome hurdles like:

- Competition in the form of other job applicants
- Faceless, nameless electronic job postings
- Faceless, nameless human resource (HR) or personnel staff

We all suffer a crisis of confidence especially when assessing our chances with the same old tools we have been taught to use from day one. You know, those time-honored tools like:

- Resumes
- Reference letters
- Cover Letters
- Referrals or references

Do they seem flat and stale? Especially in light of the tough and vibrant job market? Does it feel like you are using a dull butter knife when you should be using a scalpel? If it does, you are right.

These tools and the avenues where we seek to use them (covered later) are all becoming less and less effective with each passing day. The employers and the job market are a lot more sophisticated and demanding and thus the bar is raised for even mid-level positions, not to mention higher managerial posts.

To do the same thing as everyone else is doing is not a winning strategy! You must do something different but not only different – it must be unusually focused and effective in order to beat the job odds! The first part of doing that is to recognize the "pattern trap" that we all find ourselves in.

Ineffective Patterns That People Follow

People follow pre-established patterns because we have been trained to do so by the "experts" and teachers that taught us when we were growing up. However, patterns are only good if they produce the results you want. We know that brushing and flossing our teeth regularly keeps away cavities and tooth decay. This is an effective pattern of behavior. But what if you are doing things that are no longer effective? Why keep doing them?

The dynamics of modern job searches along with the various sieves and filters that companies utilize are destroying the effectiveness of traditional job finding tools (resumes and cover letters) and other "old school" techniques. Companies are using very sophisticated key word search algorithms on resumes which help them to be more accurate in the combination of specifications, backgrounds, skills and credentialing than ever before. **This is not good for the typical job finder.**

Reaching the hiring manager(s) and getting him/her to see you as the right candidate for the position is the ultimate end goal of anyone looking for a new job or career. Anything that doesn't help you attain that goal is just wasting your time and money. While the title of this playbook is "Forget the Resume", we aren't saying to abandon using resumes but know that this highly utilized tool for job finders is losing its power to get you where you need to go.

The company resume filters and the sheer numbers of people sending resumes for each posted job are neutralizing YOUR resume's message and impact! If you've ever been in a dangerously crowded bar, train station or rock concert where you were fighting with ten thousand other people just to get to an exit or entry then you have a pretty good picture of what is happening to your resume.

The resume is simply lost in the crushing shuffle of other legitimate applicants and people who blindly sent out resumes using the shotgun effect as we'll see in the next section. You wait in vain hoping for a notice or call back or SOMETHING!!! But nothing comes. Sound familiar?

This constant beating down effect creates a mindset of giving up or giving in to accept ANY job because what you really want is probably looking more and more unachievable. Another offshoot of this pummeling is that it prolongs your time in unemployment or underemployment status which then drains your resources - mentally, emotionally and financially.

ONE DEFINITION OF MADNESS: doing the SAME THINGS OVER AND OVER again, EXPECTING DIFFERENT RESULTS.

So it is with job finding tools and resources that don't get you results!

Chapter 2
What Doesn't Work (Anymore)

The following list of things that don't work anymore may be controversial because it flies in the face of what is commonly accepted norms for job finding resources or methods. These are things that you may, at this very moment, be doing or using. But let's examine them and find out why they don't work anymore:

 Sending out resumes and/or cover letters

Let's look at some of the media quoted statistics recently:

CASE CITING

Google gets record 75,000 resumes in a week
Bloomberg News and Bloomberg Businessweek
Published: 4:00 am, Sunday, February 6, 2011

Google flooded with resumes

After putting out the help-wanted sign last month, Google reported getting a record-high 75,000 job applications in a single week. The number of prospective employees topped a previous weekly record, set in May 2007, by 15 percent. It also was more people than the entire population of Mountain View, the company's hometown. All told, Google expects to add more than 6,000 workers in 2011, marking the biggest hiring spree in its history. It's counting on fresh engineering talent to help it push deeper into mobile services, display advertising and Internet applications.

Read more: http://www.sfgate.com/business/article/Google-gets-record-75-000-resumes-in-a-week-2460557.php#ixzz2Ikr5hzOi

CASE CITING

News and Trends in Management
Wall Street Journal
Published: 8:14 pm, Monday, February 13, 2012

Applicants Are Fewer, And Many Are Lacking

Companies are seeing fewer applicants per job opening, but recruiters say they are still seeing too many unqualified candidates.

The average number of applications submitted per job opening fell to 118 in the fourth quarter, from 187 during the same period in 2010, according to new research from the Corporate Executive Board. However, among those applicants, just 35% met the basic experience, education and skills requirements listed for the position. Previously, that figure stood at 32%.

The study, which polled more than 215 recruiters, mostly at large companies, found that "serial applicants"—job seekers who apply online to several positions in a single blast—are one reason why the job-screening process continues to be so time consuming. Recruiters take 9.5 hours, on average, to screen résumés and applications submitted for a single job opening, the study found.

Another factor is that many companies are expanding the scope of their job requirements, making positions more difficult to fill, according to Chris Ellehuus, managing director at CEB.

Hmmm. So 118 applications for a posted job is the "average" which dropped from 187 applications?

And of those numbers 65% (inverse of the 35% qualified applicants) were wasting everyone's time and clogging up the works!!

This is what happens in the real world and even though the Google example may be extreme in that it is a highly sought out company to work for – it still underscores the incredible pressure and overwhelming odds that your poor resume has to fight against just to be considered!

Networking Events

Think about the premise of going to these industry or corporate mixers and socials. Are the real hiring managers going to be there? If the real hiring managers showed up then they would probably need a presidential protection detail to guard them from being mauled by would-be applicants.

Rather, most of these events have a corporate representatives and/or recruiters behind a booth with application forms and generalized information on their company. They have no power to hire or say "yes". Ask yourself this question, "what is the point of this exercise?"

Same goes for "Speed Networking" or "Corporate Speed Dating" events as you'll see next.

PERSONAL CASE CITING

Descent Into Madness

I once stumbled into an industry speed networking located in a posh resort where corporate types that were out of work were meeting and hoping to get "hooked up" with possible employers. I didn't know this at the time.

You see, this event was part of a bigger industry-wide meeting to which my wife was invited so I was the trailing spouse. I was asked by my wife to go to Ballroom Z to deliver headache medicine for our friend who was in that ballroom doing something (it wasn't made clear to me exactly what).

When I opened the door to Ballroom Z I thought I was in the Chicago Mercantile pit - you know the area where traders are yelling at each other at full volume!! There must have been about 300 – 400 people networking like mad and having exchanged cards moving onto the next person to network at ful tilt again. It was a madhouse! If the people weren't so earnest and somewhat desperate it would have been funny or creepy.

I thought to myself, as I delivered the medicine to our friend and hurriedly left the room, what an incredibly graphic illustration of what people will put themselves through to get a shot at a job! It was something I hope I never have to do. The second thought was "how effective was that exercise"?

Job or Industry Fairs

You should be careful in approaching these events. I am not saying these events have no value but when attending them you should have a realistic expectation of what may come from them.

If your expectation is that you will get a job shortly after going to these events then your hope may be misplaced. Why? Because, once again, no real hiring managers are usually there but rather generic company representatives and/or recruiters. There are other reasons why these events may not bear much fruit:

- Soup to nuts (from extremely over talented and experienced positions to stocking grocery shelves)
- Fishing in the same tide pools as everyone else is which has the same effect as sending your resume out to a singular job posting on an electronic bulletin want ad
- Depressing in terms of numbers of people and the feeling that you are a drone – it is a downer to see the people you are running up against

The following is an example of one very enlightening if not depressing job fair I attended. I have been to other "fairs" and they all have the same dynamics and results.

PERSONAL CASE CITING

Out-gunned, Out-classed and Needing to Use the Toilet

When I first landed in Washington DC area (full story in Chapter 3), I saw a one page advertisement that stated all the defense contracting companies that were taking applications for various technical positions were coming together for a 2 day event at a local Embassy Suites. It was a kind of defense technology job fair.

I was interested in the listed companies even though I was not a techie but I wanted to know who and what was going to be there. I showed up with my briefcase full of multiple resumes and wearing my best corporate warrior outfit!

I walked into the large open atrium of Embassy Suites with the main area and certain ground floor suites occupied by various defense contracting firms. It was the Who's Who of big defense contracting firms like: Boeing, Lockheed Martin, Northrop Grumman, Raytheon, General Dynamics, SAIC, etc

At each makeshift kiosk or occupied suite there were one or two people representing the various divisions of these companies with 1-5 job application/descriptions posted for people to apply for. However there was a very practical if not brutal way of applying that these applicants had to go through.

Did I mention that at each booth, kiosk or suite there were at least 15-20 people in line? All professionals, all dressed to kill and all sizing up their potential competition with "elevator eyes".

I picked a line and stood in it to gain the real world experience of participating in one of these events.

As the line moved forward, I observed that as each applicant reached the kiosk they literally had to provide a verbal summary of their personal information about themselves and why they felt they were qualified for the posted position. All of this had to be done in a 30 second time frame and just to make sure that they kept to schedule integrity, the booth manning personnel had stopwatches!!

CONT'D

As I got closer and closer this is what I heard:

"My name is Kathryn XXXX and I worked formerly with Accenture as project leader over Project RTS which had a budget of $50 million per year and had 60 people under me. My educational background is MIT undergraduate in electrical and bio-chemical engineering…"

"Hi, my name is Tony VVVV and my background is that I graduated Cal Poly Suma Cum Laude got my masters from Stanford Magna Cum Laude. I have had 15 years in defense contract project management with my last work as director of the Excelsior project which had a budget of $200 million a year and 252 member team."

I was getting very, very nervous and feeling extremely overwhelmed by the competition. When it was my turn up at bat the company person asked me for my resume and was readying his stop watch for my spiel.

I said, "STOP!"

The man seemed stunned that I had the audacity to tell him what to do.

I then said "I have two questions for you"

"What?!" he said kind of upset that I was breaking his method of processing people

"What is the position that we are applying for?" was my first question

"Didn't you read the description?", he said visibly annoyed. "It's for a budget analyst position"

I was stunned. The description of the budget analyst position and the pay range indicated on the information sheet was way below the talents and experiences of these high flying applicants.

"Second question" I said

"What is it?" he replied

"Where's the bathroom?" I asked

"Uh- uh- uh… over there" the recruiter replied somewhat puzzled as he pointed to the loo.

I then left the kiosk and used the facilities before I left the Embassy Suites.

As I drove out in the borrowed car from the lot of the Embassy Suites facility, I called my loving and supportive wife who asked me how I was doing with the job fair. I said the following:

"I left after one booth, I'll explain later. We are so-o-o-o-o-o screwed!" We both laughed nervously.

Why am I telling you all this? Well, if this was a typical job fair (or should it be called a "cattle call"?), then it tells me that most people's experiences will be negative in the sense that they will come away with no real leads and a feeling that they are not worth a whole lot. I know I felt that way and I am notorious for having an oversized ego!

So, what are job fairs, trade and industry fairs and diversity fairs good for? Principally, they are for intelligence gathering on the company or the industry that you are interested in. These fairs are a veritable fountain of knowledge of companies and their subsidiaries and all that they want you to know of them, all positioned in a positive light! If you go to these events don't get sucked into the need to apply or meet with the personnel at the booths or even to drop off a resume. Your time is better spent with a folio or shopping bag full of their information nicely paper clipped together for future file building (see Week 3 activities later).

Headhunter or Placement Firms

The operative thinking behind using some of these big, high profile houses or the smaller boutique shops is that these folks are experts and are dialed into the very best and sharpest firms out there and that is why you should use them to try to get a job.

However, flaw in that thinking is this IF they choose to take you on as a possible candidate and are willing to show you to their real customers, then you already are probably very hire-able and don't really need their services for much more than facilitating a possible auction war for your services between two suitor firms. Wouldn't that be a wonderful scenario?

The reality is that most companies will not pay 1-2 months (or more) of salary for a mid-grade or even high grade salary ($100k or more) unless they could not get that through specialized means. Stop and think. Why would you (as an employer) pay such a hefty commission fee for something that you could post on Monster.com or Careerbuilder.com or theLadders.com sites for practically free and get a tsunami wave of candidates? Oh sure, you would be inundated with soup to nuts but that is what the HR or personnel departments are there for, right?

Same for job fairs and want ads in general, the employers want the best of the best. They want a heavy duty academic history with a long and demonstrably powerful skill base and work experience coupled with advantages (i.e. specializations, client base following, unusual skills, etc) that 90% of the populace simply doesn't possess.

As an employer using headhunters, if you are shelling out that kind of money for that kind of talent then you had better be getting the top 5-8% of the marketplace. So it is understandable that the headhunter firms make the most amount of money from the absolute strongest candidates and are not interested in anyone else.

> **PRO NOTES:**
>
> *If you are thinking of changing industries or type of job then you would not be of interest to headhunters simply because they are looking for someone who is an established maven and market maker for their corporate clients. Transitional career moves are not usually welcomed.*

Family and Friends Connections

Ah yes! Now we come to the most often used resource that most of us mere mortals draw from when we are in the job finding market! Family and friends or associates! Why wouldn't we? It is safe, warm and easy. However, built into these is a serious hidden flaw.

The thinking is that we need to have connections and the fastest way is through people whom we know, love, like or (at least) are familiar with. But this route suffers from the same problem as networking events and that is that everyone is at pretty much the same level of income and/or strata.

Unless you are a Kennedy or Gates, you probably do not have access to higher end hiring. You say you don't need to have C suite leaders know you? You just want to have a hiring manager in vice president or director level to hire you? Great! Two questions: where are they and which one?

You see, with friends and families or associates you really don't have a choice as to who they know and at what company. It is "catch as catch can" as far as what you get. Unless you are very fortunate, very few higher-ups are in exactly the industry and companies you are aspiring to get into.

Even if that were the case, a lot of people including family members and friends are loathe to make recommend due to possible backlash to their jobs, careers, or reputational standing if the "match" does not go well. Sorry.

> **BEGINNER NOTES:**
>
> I need to make a confession. My first job out of college was through my eldest brother Leon who helped me to get an interview with The Lomas and Nettleton Company (a now defunct mortgage bank) which at the time was the largest mortgage bank in the world. I also wanted to cut my teeth in the financial market so this was literally a bullet hitting a bullet in midair! It has not happened since then.

Job Sites (Electronic or Want Ads)

It does not matter what you use, whether it be: Monster.com, Careerbuilder.com, theLadders.com, FINS.com or the local, regional, national newspapers they all follow a certain pattern. They are all massive collators and aggregators of job candidates. This presents a series of obstacles that you need to overcome in order to get to the hiring manager.

 Obstacle 1:

Indiscriminate collation with little pre-screening or with super-tight key word search algorithm of tsunami-like wave of applications which contain valid and legitimate applications that actually have a shot at the positions (like yours) mixed in with job posting "serial applicants" who will apply for anything. The average recruiter spends 9.5 hours sifting through all this to glean a few candidates that may be interviewed. (See WSJ article from earlier section for additional detail)

 Obstacle 2:

We've all been in companies and seen jobs posted internally first which then go out shortly thereafter for external posting. There is a tendency for most firms to hire from within for good reasons (knowledge of the culture, ways of doing things and a "known" element). Usually the internal candidates have a pretty strong chance of getting these jobs.

 Obstacle 2a:

A corollary problem to the above scenario is that the externally posted jobs are usually posted because they cannot be filled internally and so the skills of the external candidate are of a higher end nature, which is fine but this new external focus then pulls in very sharp, smart folks who may have resumes that outshine yours (that does NOT mean that these people are better at the position than you might be).

 Obstacle 3:

Jobs posted are not necessarily where you want to go in terms of career direction, location, or type of work requested. They are typically fairly random in nature.

 Obstacle 4:

Want ads vacillate from top end (cardiac surgeon, CEO) to low end (janitor, warehouse worker) with a huge nursing or medical technician section. But what about the thick middle layer of workers which is where most people inhabit?

Reality CHECK

Yes it is true that someone you know (maybe even you) may have gotten jobs through these methods because if that weren't true then all these sources would dry up due to disillusioned applicants and burned employers. A lot of effort and time has been spent by a lot of people on these sites with little or no payoff. However, this playbook is about stacking the odds in your favor and approaching the market on a less trampled path.

I knew a friend who applied for 200 positions and only got 2 call backs. Both were 100% commission sales which is a no-brainer type risk for the types of companies that post for these types of positions since they are not obligated to pay a base salary.

 ### Obstacle 5 (the biggest one):

If you do get past the filters and get a call back then you will be going through an intermediary such as Personnel or Human Resource departments. You will probably not be preliminarily meeting with the key hiring manager. These people have the power to say NO but not the ability to say YES. The point of your efforts is to get in front of the ultimate decision maker.

Okay, now that I've thoroughly depressed you with these examples let me tell you my story of the very last time I used these ineffective resources we covered.

I will tell you what I did :

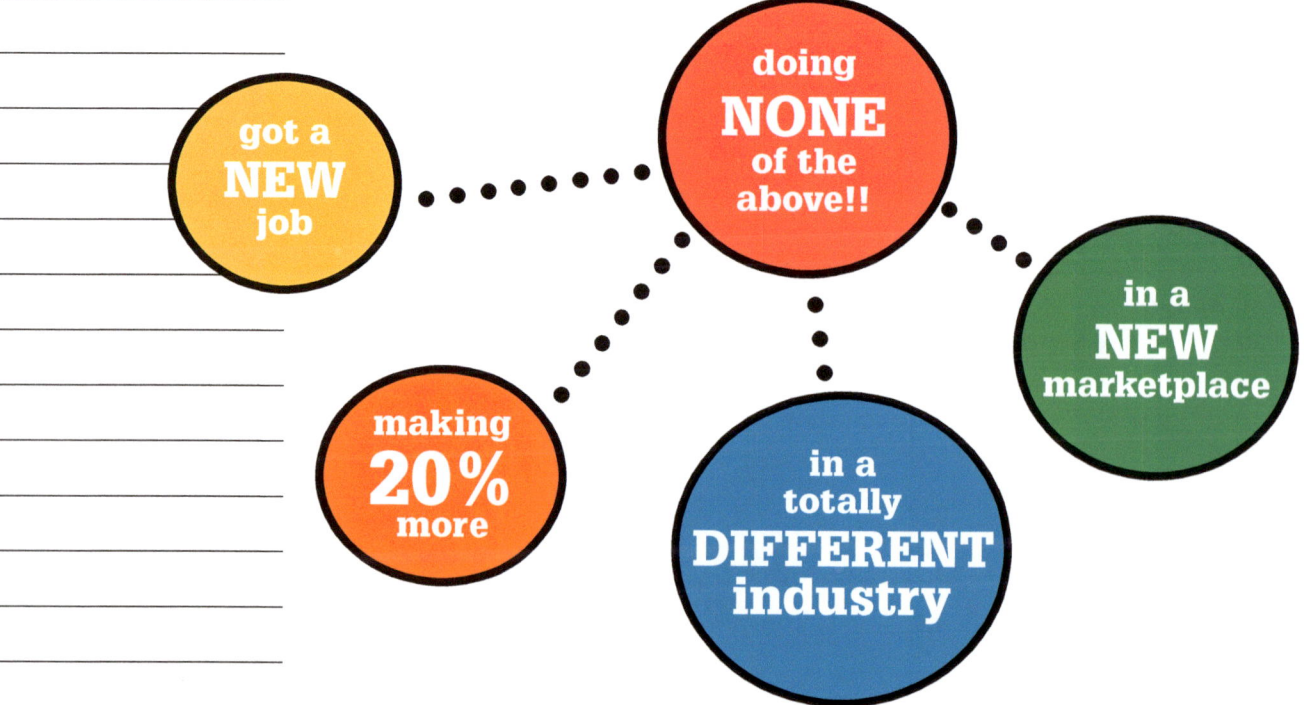

Chapter 3
Desperation = Inspiration

I went through a really hard time in my life starting in 2001 and going through 2002. I was 41 and it was September of 2002. My project work as a fundraiser for a great seminary (Northwest Theological Seminary located in Lynnwood, Washington) was winding down. I took this fundraising job in September 2001 as a hiatus from the corporate world because I was burnt out from 20 years of toil. Then,

9/11 hit and businesses and people stopped giving charitable contributions.

I was diagnosed with a rare form of leukemia.

My world bottomed out as I went through a lot of pain from the cancer and the chemotherapy.

With the support of the seminary's great leaders and my loving wife and family, I was in remission as of mid-2002. So now what? Well, I've always wanted to live on the east coast having been a Seattle boy for all my formative years. I pushed it off saying "tomorrow or next year" but after leukemia I realized that life could be unbelievably short. After talking it over with my wife Sandy, we moved with our young son Preston to the Washington DC area to pound out a new life.

We landed in a suburb of DC and I assessed the situation:

1. Moved from Seattle to Washington DC area
2. Need to support myself and wife and a young son
3. No job prospects
4. No connections (viable ones that is)
5. Wanting to do something totally different (in another industry).

I had a nine month burn rate of my funds until we hit the WALL (that is to say, living under a bridge eating pork and beans or worse). Having gone to all the following places to conduct my job searching, I became very sad and panicky.

- Classified (want) ads of major newspapers
- Recruiting firms (head hunters)
- Job and trade fairs
- Jobs online through job sites such as: Hotjobs.com , Monster.com, Careerbuilder.com
- Networking functions (in various industries)
- Friends and families' connections

Can you feel the level of despair that I was experiencing? So after spending 5 months trying these traditional routes and wasting precious time, a cold sweat panic start to descend upon me as I came to the very frightening realization that all these traditional or "safe" methods were going nowhere FAST!!

One thought (a challenge actually) came to me – if I thought of myself as a master sales and marketing person (having been in those fields for 20 years) then shouldn't I be able to sell the product I knew best which was me?! That challenge coupled with the fact that I had 4 more months to go till I hit the wall prompted me to re-think my way of approaching the marketplace when looking for a job!

Instead of treating this as a "job finding" or "job search" task, I started to think of it as a very important product launch into the job (business) market. Drawing from my background in sales and marketing I did a re-think of the WHOLE situation. The product was me and the product launch into the job market needs to be (like all launches) well researched, targeted and results producing!

Sequentially, these were the steps I took:

Step 1:

Instead of sending out hundreds of resumes blindly so as to increase my "exposure" to the employers out there, what I did was concentrate on 15 employers, and that's it. I wanted to get into the security world (something that I had no previous experience in whatsoever) based upon the location that where I lived – Washington DC. I knew there were (still are) a lot of mammoth defense contractors in that part of the world! I surfed the net on the new hot topics of the defense contracting world and happened upon a project called Operation Safe Commerce (OSC) funded by the Department of Homeland Security . OSC had some of the largest defense contracting companies on the planet participating in OSC.

Step 2:

I used the OSC list of participating companies as the main backbone of my target list for potential employment. I then started to learn about Operation Safe Commerce which was an initiative to secure ocean containers coming into the United States post 9/11. This was an interesting crossover because I did have an extensive background in logistics especially ocean container movement. Hmmmm...

Step 3:

In compiling the list of 15 OSC participating companies, I separated these companies into top 5, mid 5 and bottom 5. Some of the companies on the list were: Boeing, Raytheon, SAIC, Lockheed Martin, Pinkerton Consulting and Investigations, Unisys, CH2M Hill, etc. I then researched the top 5 of the list (the companies that I thought were the most promising for whatever reason I thought at the time).

I concentrated on the C suite leadership (CEO, COO, CFO) of these targeted companies.

Step 4:

In my research of the OSC project I kept running into a term called RFID. RFID was an acronym for Radio Frequency Identification tagging which was an emerging leading edge technology that was a hot topic in both the security and supply chain world because Walmart Corporation had just stated that they would be interested in a cost effective RFID system to be used in their business. WHOA!! Everyone took notice after that announcement. I wrote a position paper from the research that I gathered because I needed to be smart about this topic when I talked to anyone from the OSC list.

See Exhibit 1: John Lee's Position Paper Version 1: Unysis

My thinking was that I knew a lot about supply chain having been in it for 9 years and now RFID (the hot topic) and OSC were helping to bridge the two worlds of supply chain and security! WOW!

But I didn't want to talk to low level folks. I wanted to engage at as high of a level as I could.

So, who's higher than the CEO? I read Anthony Parinello's *Selling to VITO* book two years ago and his audacious method struck and stuck with me. In his sales book, Parinello showed how to get a hold of the C suite executive of a company to get a meeting and start the dialogue. It was a selling book but, hey, I am selling myself as a "product" wasn't I?

Step 5:

After a point in the researching, I made a cold call script and then I called Boeing's main line and asked for then CEO Phil Condit. I don't mind telling you that I was sweating! But miraculously I was sent through to Mr. Condit's assistant. I was stunned!! And when I was asked about the nature of the call I stuttered out the fact that I wanted to talk to the person who was in charge of supply chain security within the company. This very helpful assistant gave me the name and number of the executive vice president of that division. I thanked her and hung up. I then called the named executive vice president armed with Mr. Condit's assistant's name and I invoked it by truthfully saying that I was referred to him by her.

I did not know if this gambit would work until I got a call from that executive vice president a few hours later!! When asked the meaning or purpose of the call I told him I wanted to know if he could point me to the ACTIONABLE person within his division with whom I could talk about possibilities to do work with them either on a fulltime or contract basis. To my furthering amazement – he gave me his director's name and phone number!!! I thanked him, hung up and collapsed onto my couch!!

I had two competing emotions at this time. One was relief due to the nervousness that was pent up and the other was excitement because I believed I had finally found the way to effectively and decisively punch through the wall of "no's" that I had encountered with the traditional methods.

I then proceeded to knock down the other four targeted companies using this method and sure enough they all played out accordingly! I then went through the whole list of companies (15 altogether) in the next 3 weeks to set up meetings for informational or exploratory interviews!

 I want you to know that not all of the calls were successful or led to anything. However, all the work that I put into researching the companies and the position paper, etc had paid off more than all the job sites, want ads, job fairs, etc ever produced! I met real hiring managers that were willing to look at this newbie as a possibility for hire.

Step 6:

Every time I met with someone talking about RFID and its uses I kept on asking if there were possible positions opening up or existing where I could be considered. Eight companies discussed the possibilities of me working for them and all were hiring managers or at the very least a member of the hiring team.

If the people I contacted couldn't meet me then I would mail them my position paper and have them look it over. I then circled back with them to see if they read it and asked them to meet with me. Most of them agreed to meet me.

NOTE: I never sent in my resume with the position paper!! I would only give my resume if I met with the hiring managers and only at the end of the meeting.

Why? Because resumes are a dime a dozen in the hiring world. They also don't allow the hiring manager to see what you have to offer in terms of: original ideas, ability to convey those ideas well, and level of care and preparedness that is necessary in a well constructed thought capital set piece.

NOTE: My position paper was becoming more complex and had more layers than the original one.

See Exhibit 1: John Lee's Position Paper Version 2&3 Pinkerton

Results:

I had active dialogues with multiple hiring managers within those 8 targeted firms about the prospects of me working for them. From the first of these meetings and onward, I was armed with the position paper (I had a copy of my resume for backup).

The outcome is that I had two job offers and I took the best of the two which was Unisys Corporation's offer. Bottom line is that through this process, I accomplished many things at once:

1. I transitioned into a job that was in supply chain security (new industry)
2. I got a 20% increase in pay from my previous West Coast jobs (which helped immensely as DC was a lot more expensive than Seattle)
3. I got affirmation of a system that has proven itself time and time again throughout my personal and business life (I use it for reaching clients that are hard to reach)
4. I didn't have to live under the bridge eating pork and beans! After the initial 5 months wasted doing traditional method, I took this new approach which produced a great job offer in 4 months time. If you recall I had a 9 month burn rate till we hit the wall. God is Great!

 There are NO guarantees of timeframe or results using this method but I believe that when you actually put the FTR Career System into action you will see things happen in a real way!

*NOTE: This chapter is excerpted and modified from my book **The Honorable Relationship** - available at Amazon.com.*

PS - The funny thing was that some of the employers were still interested in me after I went with my first choice (Unisys) and we continued to dialogue throughout my tenure at Unisys. Eventually, a superior offer came from one of those conversations (Pinkerton Consulting) and I took it with a pay jump of 25% and a vice president title.

PPS – Please note that I was creating all this on an ongoing basis having never done this type of job finding technique EVER!! I have since then refined this process as you will see next.

Chapter 4
Template for What Really Works

This section previews the process for the Forget the Resume (FTR) Career System will lead you through.

The point of all your hard work is to get the RIGHT job in the RIGHT company that is in the RIGHT industry. You can substitute "right" for "appropriate". So how do you do that?

You've got to think in a radically different way than ever before. Start off by not thinking of this as a job search but as a product launch with you as the "product".

I have done many product launches in my life; the idea is to tailor the product presentation to the right audience who are going to actually purchase the product. You as the "product" have a defined set of skills, talents, education, experience and interests which can be of great value and use to others but who are these "others" and how can you paint an accurate and flattering picture of your great value?

There is no sense in launching, say, men's deodorant products to an audience of teen girls. That would be a horrendous waste of time! Great marketers first look at the potential markets its product is best suited for in order to understand the needs and uses of the product in the context of the buyer's perspective.

So the first step is to find the markets that you are interested in pursuing AND that will reward your skills.

A. Create your own FTR Career System by doing the following:

1. Industry focus - Look at 1 or 2 industries that are interesting for you. These could be the one you are already in or something different. If it is a different industry, you really must consider what skills, experience or talent you have that would translate well to this new industry. If you don't have the requisite skills and making the move would require additional training, don't rule it out but keep that under consideration.

2. Within the 1 or 2 industries you are researching, create a list of the companies that are the top 12 desirable companies in those industries.

 This part requires realism. If you have a high school diploma and you are interested in a position as an operations manager of a bio-genetics company, you probably are not going to get very far. The point is NOT to waste time trying to make something fit which is simply not going to work.

As you research the initial top 12 firms that you are interested in, create a file folder (electronic and hardcopy please) for each of them. In the actual Week 3 section dealing with this process I will roll out the structure on what and how the information will look like.

3. Find the 2 top associations that are linked with these industry(ies) and join them to leverage industry information and also for the ability to meet with industry connectors. Every industry has "connectors" who are basically people who are genetically hot-wired to know a lot of people by sheer personality and interests. This is a term that Malcolm Gladwell used in *The Tipping Point* and they definitely exist!

Do not join associations that are not the major associations for the industry(ies) that you are interested in. See if there are top level titles and or names that are on their member roster.

Please don't just go to the network mixers. I'll cover more later in Week 2 but you've got to really invest some time and effort into these associations for them to really pay off in helping you in your job finding and after you do get the job – in your career!

B. Write a Position Paper.

What is a position paper? It is a well researched but brief (1-2 pages at the beginning) of a topic or trend that is very "hot" or much talked about in the industry(ies) that you are targeting.

This is very, very important because you are really going to use this as the talking point and entry card to get in to talk to the prospective hiring managers of the targeted firms that you picked to pursue.

The main reason why this is important is that the position paper shows your thought process and ability to present your thoughts on a topic that interests the hiring managers. It is not like a resume which only tells people what you have done up to now but rather it gives them a glimpse of the real person behind the piece of paper.

Helping Hint:
In the case of my situation I chose the idea of security in the supply chain and the effect of RFID in that world.

Still do have a well prepared resume (forget the cover letter – nobody reads these anymore) but the resume is only used at certain points in time which will be explained later).

✓ If you are not a good writer then please seek help either from a familiar person who is good at it (friend or family) or get a professional to help you write it. The research and ideas have got to be from YOU however, because you really have to "own" the topic and know it well in order to speak to it during your upcoming interviews.

Reality CHECK

Also, take a definite position – don't just regurgitate information or articles. Remember, this is not just writing a stupid term paper for school, this is a tool to get you past other applicants as you show your thought process and ideas. So show some direction and voice your opinion in the paper – there will be samples of position papers and how they can evolve later in the Week 2 section. Don't be arrogant about it but leave room and space for differing opinions.

C. Use your FTR Career System

Now comes the time where you will be using all the various tools you've created to engage with the market. This part may seem scary at first but you will get the hang of it and the fear factor will go away very quickly. This method I call the Fearless Method, in fact. What is your next step here? You need to call the CEO or an equivalently high level officer of the companies you have targeted. Remember the list of the formidable companies I had (Boeing, Raytheon, General Dynamics, etc)?

Please know that you don't have to be a fast talker with smooth words. What you need (and I have included a script to follow and use) is courage. Remember, courage is not the absence of fear but the overcoming of it!

Your purpose is NOT to talk to the CEO but to get his assistant's name (I'll explain later) and have him/her guide you to where you need to go in the company that works with the subject topic you are interested in.

Using the Fearless Method is the most effective way of getting to the right hiring manager. The problem in getting to the right manager especially in a very large firm is being able to find him/her and then to make them sufficiently interested in talking to you. How do you do sift through a company population that can range from 1,000 to 10,000 to 100,000 people strong? It is like finding a needle in 1,000 haystacks especially in the virtual work environment where we all live. If you start at the top with their level of visibility, you can be pointed in the right direction and everyone on the way down to the hiring manager knows the direction from where you were sent that is, from the next level higher than themselves. For a visualization of the problem at hand, consider the illustration:

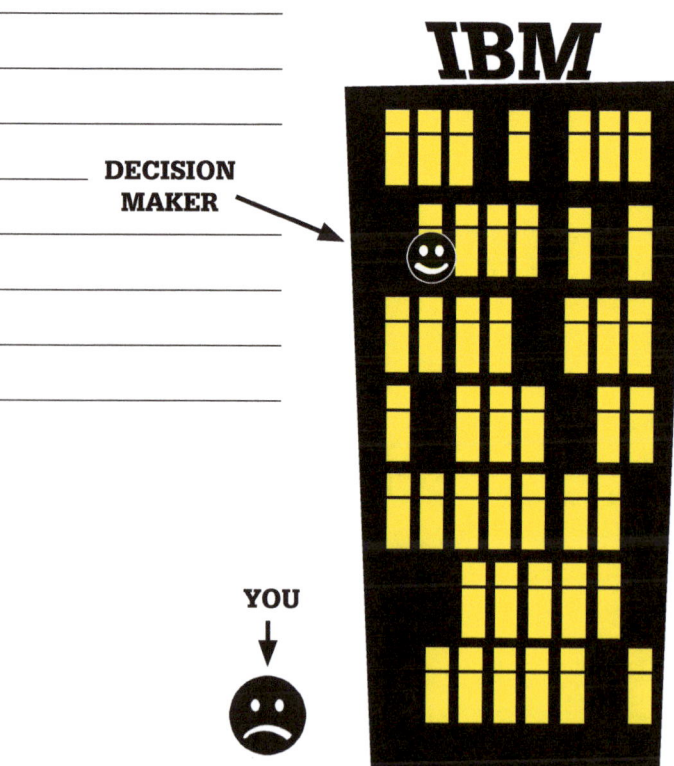

NOTE: *International Business Machines Corporation (IBM) is used strictly for illustrative purposes. IBM's employee and contractor population are in the tens of thousands spread throughout the world and having various reporting structures (direct versus indirect). Illustration excerpted from The Honorable Relationship available from Amazon.com*

While this may make you nervous (who can blame you) please know that it works and this is about your economic survival! This method helps to cut through a lot of crap that is intentionally put up to block people from reaching the hiring manager.

This is why the Fearless Method is so effective in not only getting to the right person but incentivizing him/her to call you back by leveraging the CEO's office's influence to help open doors.

There are other ways such as:

- Engaging with the head of a department (you'll need to get him/her to talk to you by going through the CEO's office)
- Association within the targeted industries
- Connectors within the targeted associations

These informational interviews will give you two things. First they will give you more information to refine your existing position paper. Second, and more importantly, they will show that person that you have your lights on and are enthusiastic, sincere and driven in pursuit of a job within their firm.

Helping Hint:
When you talk to a higher level person (VPs or directors) about the position paper's topic take notes like crazy. Write down what the main points of what they are saying. DON'T DEPEND UPON YOUR MEMORY and no it is not rude. Actually they will be very impressed with the fact that you are paying such attention!

Stop! Let's take a break from this lest you think that this method is for Super People only who are already really good at sales or are outgoing! Read Chapter 5 which introduces my nephew Darren and the story of how he got his first corporate job after college using the FTR Career System.

Chapter 5
Darren's Story

Before we dive in to the FTR program, I think it is important for you to see what someone without corporate or business experience background can do when using the FTR Career System.

Darren is my nephew and in September 2007 I got a call from him asking me for ideas to get a job. I was a bit stunned to hear this because I thought that Darren had already started the process but he had not. In talking through the situation, I assessed that Darren was thinking of using the traditional routes of resume and cover letter writing, job sites, trolling job sites, attending job fair, blah blah ad nausem.

So I simply asked him "do you want to do the traditional method and all that it entails or do you want to treat finding a job like a job and do something very radical but that is effective?" After some thought, Darren decided to hear more about this "radical" new method.

I sent Darren a very long email detailing all the things that he needed and the process by which to do it. This has all been further refined in this playbook. Among one of the exhibits I sent him was a spreadsheet of a week's schedule for the first 2 weeks.

See Exhibit 3: The Serious Jobfinders Schedule - Darren's Version

As Darren started the process, I remembered he was a bit fearful of the eventual outcome because he was spending a lot of time setting things up, assembling materials, and researching companies, industries and topics. I sensed he had doubts about my methods especially in light of the generally accepted routes to take. However, to his credit, Darren stayed with the program!

Initially, Darren was interested in pursuing a marketing position with a video game company. The topic he liked was in-game advertising (IGA) which in 2007 was a very hot topic in the industry. He did this by canvassing the internet from industry leaders and sources.

After the initial weeks, I was duly impressed by the position paper he wrote regarding the topic of IGA.

See Exhibit- Darren's Position Paper Version 3

It was about this time that Darren was ready to engage with the Top 12 targeted firms because he had done a lot of information gathering already. Darren started with the Top 4 firms (of his choice) and began to call the CEOs.

Darren was very nervous prior to the first call (to the point where he had to throw up) but after cleaning up he resolved to make the call. He reached the CEO's administrative assistant and requested help from her to send him to the appropriate silo head who turned out to be a vice president.

I remember how excited Darren was when he told me of the first call's results which was that the CEO's administrative assistant led to the business unit's vice president who then directed Darren to the next rung lower (director). This was not a small company in the video gaming world.

Emboldened by the results, Darren moved forward to contact the other 3 companies on his Top 4 targeted companies then on to his Mid 4 companies and later his Low 4 companies.

Here are the results of Darren's hard work:

Interviewed with:	Had Chats With:	Contacted:

Expedia
    multiple interviews
    job offer
	Microsoft	Sony

Google
    Flown down to Austin ,TX
    multiple interviews
	Aquantive – online advertising	Nintendo

Electronic Arts / EA Phone interview	Ubisoft – video game publisher	Ascentium
Publicis West – Advertising	Activision – video game publisher	Sega
BDA Inc. – Promotional Merchandising	Valve Corporation – video game developers (in person)	Lucasarts
DDB – advertising	Wongdoody – advertising	Namco Bandai
Horton Lantz & Low	DraftCB Seattle – advertising	Capcom
KMPS - Country radio station	Comcast Spotlight - advertising	Take 2
Alltar Directory	Hawkeye -- advertising	Sedgewick Rd
	Worktank – advertising	DNAbm
	Enterprise Seattle – government – stimulate game industry	Don't Blink
	Encore Media Group	Konami
	Paradigm Events	Massive
	Sandlot Games	THQ
	Facebook	T-Mobile
		Bungie
		Vivendi Universal
		Zombie Studios

BEGINNER NOTES:

You'll notice that Darren has gone beyond the initial 12 but when he started it was with Top 12 video game publishers. Afterward, Darren ventured into Top 12 for regional advertising companies and technology based firms

Darren followed the FTR Career System religiously and worked it as it should which was to work hard, smart and professionally; basically he was treating looking for a job as a job.

The results were stunning! One director of a video game publisher who spoke with Darren was wondering how Darren knew so much about his company and the industry better than many executives and business people he had spoken with through all the years he'd been with the firm!

The director went on further to say that he consented to meet with Darren after reading the position paper to accomplish two things: first, assess Darren's experience level and second, to find out if he had ever worked in a video gaming environment before and how Darren was able to write such an accurate and detailed assessment about his company.

In March 2008 Darren accepted a job offer from Expedia. If you are paying attention, it took six months but this is after adding two new industries (internet and advertising) to the original video gaming industry and having done a thorough canvassing of all the companies that he was interested in. Considering that Darren had no prior work experience (other than two short internships) he was happy with the results.

Chapter 6
A Fresh New Start

The approach to the product launch of YOU is done through 3 major avenues with a very powerful tool! The reason why it is a multi-pronged attack is because in the rough and tumble world of job acquisition you just don't know what will work and when.

- **Approach #1: The Fearless Method** – calling the CEO or head of the company/firm/organization to leverage his/her office (not the CEO themselves but the power of his/her office) to identify where you need to go and who to talk to. Obtaining the name of the CEO's administrative assistant is key for this process to work!!

- **Approach #2: The Power of Associations** – joining the premier association(s) of the industry or field/discipline you are targeting to get to the decision makers and influencers and begin meaningful dialogue which then enhances your chances of referrals with references. Another side benefit is to get industry specific knowledge that makes you look smart and sharp.

- **Approach #3: The connectors** - a person who is in the industry and knows a lot of people.

- **Tool for Approach:** A well researched and written position paper on a hot topic or subject

In doing these 3 things you are really hedging your bets so that you have maximum coverage and stickiness in getting the product launched - which is **YOU**.

Outline of the Forget the Resume Career System
(when you are done with the 6 week program you will have completed the following):

Short term (1-3 weeks) goals/outcomes are:

- Get your FTR Career System up and running (with resources, systems and costs all in place)
- Industries, associations for targeting identified and researched
- Position paper on hot topic or trend identified and researched
- Top 12 companies identified + alternate 4 companies
  (Top 4 companies, Mid 4 companies, Low 4 companies) + alternate 4 companies

Mid term (4-5 weeks) goals/outcomes are:

- Practice and engage with Top 4 companies' targeted personnel with Fearless Method
- Meet with associations and join boards or committees to get deeper industry relationships
- Canvas for influencers, connectors, and decision makers
- Refine the position paper

Long term (6 weeks – 3 or 4 months) goals are:

- Pursue the targets and arrange meetings (informational or otherwise)
- Send off the position papers in lieu of resume for folks that don't want to meet initially
- Get into the rhythm of meeting and narrowing in on existing jobs or un-posted positions

  NOTE: Get in front of a company prior to a job posting – once it is posted your probability of being hired goes down sharply

PERSONAL CASE CITING

Interviewing for "Non-existing" Jobs

In my lifetime, I have gotten 3 jobs that were just about to be posted (but had not been posted yet) and I have gotten 3 jobs that were brand new positions that were being contemplated for launch but they weren't clear as to what candidate type they needed until I showed up.

You may say "he's just incredibly lucky" but I prefer the "The harder I work, the luckier I get" because most of these positions came from informational interviews and in the process of asking well-researched questions I struck someone's interest. But you have to talk to the right manager which is to say, hiring manager!

When you meet with hiring managers who are interested in you then the probability of getting you into the firm goes up exponentially! (This is what happened to Darren as well). This internal, personal "champion" of your cause may be the person who eventually hires you or refers you to someone else who could hire you.

Helping Hint:

Here is a weird-but-true fact of human behavior – if you ask very well researched questions then the person that is responding to these questions begins to think that you are a smart and sharp individual even if most of the time you spend together is in asking questions. I know it sounds weird but when I have interviewed applicants it was the individuals who asked good questions and pursued answers a little more past my responses that impressed me most!

Chapter 7
Week 1 - Preparation

START
Week 1 Goals:

We will go through this together – it's not easy but not that hard either! We will go through the 6 weeks with a standard format of checklist, to do's, and actions review.

Checklist:

- ☒ Get your mindset re-set so that you know and are committed to this System
- ☒ Get into a serious mindframe of the discipline you will need to get what you want!
- ☒ Get resources (most everything) in place for you to begin your FTR Career System
- ☒ Create a workable job finding schedule that mimics work schedules complete with lunch break and 2 breaks a day from 8:30 am to 5 pm

Week 1 To-Do's:
Mindset Changes

You must, must, must do the following before anything else! Re-train your brain to think in the following manner.

Mindset Change #1:
YOU CANNOT AFFORD TO THINK AND DO THINGS LIKE YOU USED TO!

Please understand that if you waste time or half ass this process then you will reduce the FTR Career System down to nothing! You will have wasted precious time and resources and hurt yourself in the process. You got a resume done - great. You'll use it later but it is NOT the centerpiece for this process. Lose the cover letter – nobody looks at this! The other stuff like looking at job postings, going to job fairs – forget them! **Please stop doing this!!!**

Mindset Change #2:
DO NOT MAKE EXCUSES OR DELAY THINGS!

Now that you have reached this section regardless of what time of the week - you may start! Begin by getting the materials needed below! From this section on, you can read the weeks as they occur. You don't need to read ahead if you choose not to but it may be advisable. Start the actual Week 1 on the next Monday coming up so you can keep to schedule integrity!

Mindset Change #3:
TREAT LOOKING FOR A JOB AS A JOB

Your internal outlook severely impacts your external persona. If you dress in sweatpants, sweatshirt and bunny slippers then (please believe me) you will be less business like in your attitude and discipline. Treat this period as if you were on the job. See the next section called Schedule of Success.

Mindset Change #4:
TAKE NO SHORTCUTS DOING THIS FTR CAREER SYSTEM

You will seriously mess up the way this works if you take shortcuts or try to consolidate or trim things or processes out! If you have ever baked a cake from scratch and fudged in any of the steps or combining them to make it more efficient, then you'll know that the outcomes are usually disastrous!

Trust me, FTR Career System is not perfect but it has been refined many, many times to drive out crap. Since it charts unexplored territory for you; it is critical that "you not wander too far from the old scout when camping in grizzly territory".

Get the Gear!

You probably have all the things you need to get the FTR Career System up and running but let's review just in case:

Right Now Purchases

- [x] Computer with printer or access to computer if you don't have it. (with nice print results - if not then have it printed out at retail shops)
- [x] Manila file folders (30-40 of them)
- [x] Pens/Post_Its or generic sticky notes
- [x] Organizer (Day-Timer, Franklin Covey – just to name a few)
- [x] Postage stamps – one roll of 100 stamps

Mid-term Purchases (Week 4 and 5):

- [x] Buy some new clothes (shirt/blouse, shoes, etc for work) and wear them.

Helping Hint:

This is done for two reasons: one is to update your look if you haven't gotten anything new for some time and the other is to give yourself a lift psychologically. People just feel better when they get a new "something" especially if it makes them look better.

Get new briefcase or folder for work

✓ This is done so you have a sharp, crisp professional look. If you don't have the funds for this then borrow someone else's case

Get a calling card (in lieu of a business card) –
200 cards initially through online or office supply stores. It should be easy to read with your name, mobile number and email address.

Helping Hint:
Make the design of calling cards plain with no cutesy or artsy things on it! You may like dramatic colors or cool designs but save them for your friends.

Thank you cards – best to be handwritten if you have legible handwriting

Helping Hint:
Thank you cards should be used for people who have met you (interviewers), helped you (administrative assistants) and people you've met at association meetings or events like that. Keep it short "Thank you so much for your time and guidance" "Thank you for your great help!" Print neatly if you have terrible handwriting. In doubt? Ask your spouse or special "other" for assistance.

✓ You would be amazed at the power of these thank you cards when you use them. You are remembered in a very positive way especially by administrative assistants who are the gate keepers for any executive or manager!

Starbucks cards - $5 per card – get 4 cards for upcoming follow ups

Helping Hint:
Be careful with this one. Don't just send these out indiscriminately or you'll either be broke or give the wrong impression. These cards should be given when:

An administrative assistant has gone out of his/her way (called you back several times on behalf of his/her boss to set up meetings that keep on moving, for example)

NOTE: I usually write: "After trying to get the meeting set up with Mr. Jones and me, I think you deserve a coffee break! Thank you so much!"

OR

If there is a really hard to get manager that is not able to meet (but willing to meet) due to his/her schedule.

NOTE: I usually write: "I would love to have a conversation with you over coffee. Please tell me what is a good date/time/location? Thank you"

Schedule of Success

See Exhibit 4: The Serious Jobfinder's Schedule - Blank w/ Notes

Early day:	Get up early (6 or 7 am) and clean up
	Get dressed in business casual clothing
	Get breakfast at home (something quick)
	Get your favorite beverage
	Go to your desk that you've got setup with computer, mobile phone, comfortable chair and supplies
Mid day:	Start work at 8 am or 8:30 am and don't end till 5 pm or 5:30 pm
	Organize your days to allow 3-4 uninterrupted hours of work
	Daily routine: Lunch (1 hr) and two breaks (20 minutes) – one in morning and afternoon
	Go outside during lunch to refresh and rejuvenate – do this also for breaks
NOTE:	Don't have a show or movie or TV or video game or live streaming during the work time. It is fine to have non-disruptive music kept low volume in background. Avoid distractions.
Late day:	Finish notes on research
	Make notations on follow ups for tomorrow and beyond
	Arrange work time per week to be 40 - 50 hrs
Weekends:	Take sometime to revamp or tighten up the position paper
	Clean up on some notes
	Revamp or writeup plan for the next week
	R-E-L-A-X!!! You deserve it!

Consider Target Industries

Take all the time necessary to really consider what 1 or 2 industries you want to target to enter (or stay in) because next week you will need to get the research up and running on them.

Consider which companies interest you within those 1 or 2 industries.

End – Week 1 Actions Review:
Checklist of Accomplishments:

- [x] Get materials in place to carry out your upcoming tasks
- [x] Have a "work week" schedule that you have begun to start the process
- [x] Think about 1 - 2 target industries
- [x] Compile initial list of possible 20 firms that you would be interested in the 2 target industries

Chapter 8
Week 2 - Research Industries and Topics

Start – Week 2 Goals:

A fair amount of work coming up for this week but you can do it! Now that you are setup for starting the FTR Career System, let's get started!

Checklist:

Get two crucial things done by end of week:

- [x] Research, analyze and choose 1-2 industries that you will target to enter
- [x] Research, analyze and choose the top 2 associations affiliated with the industries you chose
- [x] Write a position paper on "hot" topic/trend or innovation in the 1 or 2 industries you chose

Week 2 To Do's:
Research Industries

When researching the 1 or 2 industries that you are interested in consider, first of all, why you are interested in them to begin with - Are you in the same industry as the ones you have chosen (automotive, aviation, consumer product goods, for example)? Are you choosing different aspects of the same industry (ie., you are currently a mortgage loan processor thinking of getting into underwriting)?

Some people are interested in a function that falls into many industries such as, for example, a human resources' compensation analyst in an internet company transitioning into financial services.

Whatever the combination of possibilities the question remains why are you seeking the change? You need to be able to ask and answer in a credible fashion because the people interviewing will ask and if you are not sure or come across as flaky then it simply won't work.

A corollary question is: how much of a stretch is there to transition from what I was doing to what I want to do? If you were an auto mechanic who now wants to do currency arbitraging or brain surgery it could be a stretch! Not to put down auto mechanics – it could be the other way around and still be quite improbable.

Is there any specialized training or education required? Are there changing industry dynamics that would make what you currently are doing more viable? Remember the transition piece for me to go from supply chain background to security was the OSC project which needed expertise in supply chain to carry out the program for a lot of the defense contractors.

Forget the Resume • 39

> *NOTE: If this simply is not the case but you are still interested then fine but be aware that it helps to have something to bridge from where you are now to where you want to go.*

Other considerations:

- Sustainability of the industries – are you interested in compact disc manufacturing? If so, then it may not be for long.
- Major company players and products in the industries – who are the 800 lb gorillas in the field?
- Major trends and forecasts of the industries – what do the "experts" say about the trends in your industries of interest?
- What are the main associations (top 2) of the industries – who and what are they?
- Who are the main connectors (go-to mavens) that are often quoted?

Research Associations

Once you have chosen the industry(ies) that interest you, the next step is to find out more about the very powerful tool of associations. Associations, especially the dominant ones in the industry, are powerful networking and leveraging vehicles. These organizations pull in the big players (companies and their employees) to many events far beyond the scope of mixers or job fairs. If you go or join associations just to go to their monthly or quarterly mixers, you are missing out on a whole lot more that these associations can do! We'll cover more in just a little while about their hidden power but first here's what to look for when you do the research:

- What makes up the member base? Is it low level personnel? Mid level? High level? A combination of any of these personnel? Get as much information as you can
- Is it discipline driven (attorneys, radiologists, teachers) or is it industry driven (aviation, hospitality, petroleum)?
- What are the costs to join in terms of money (upfront and renewals), time commitments, and resources? Do you have to be nominated or recommended by someone in order to join?
- Can you join at all? If so then as what status? Are there any restrictions on your new membership?
- Can you go to meetings? What type and frequency?
- Can you serve on boards or committees? Especially ones that no one really wants like fundraising?

> ✓ **Reality CHECK**
> This is a very important part of the FTR Career System matrix of tools but will require time and energy on your part. Associations are by nature aggregators of industry folks who have points in common and that is where you should be spending time so that even though you may be an outsider, with time and familiarity you will begin to be known as an industry regular or insider. This is an investment in your CAREER and not just another JOB!

The Hidden Power of Associations

The overall goal is to meet and know industry players and learn more information about the career and industry that you are embarking on especially as it pertains to leading edge topics and ideas. If you are just going to mixers or generic networking events, you may not meet the "real" players of the industry. Why not? Well, does it make sense that if you are a C-suite officer of a company or a high level vice president or director, you would go to a come-one, come-all event? I have attended many large association functions, with differing industries, and I've never seen these high level players there.

And if these rare power brokers are there, they invariably have an entourage that "mobs" them and you are never really going to punch through effectively to deliver your elevator speech on how great you are.

Where you get REAL TRACTION with an association is in the boring and mundane business of getting onto and then serving on a committee or board within that association. These committees or boards are where you can have real exposure and one-on-one time so that you can begin to shine. Most boards or committees are full, especially the high profile ones. However, the ones that usually have vacant slots and really need help in are the ones that will give you the opportunity to serve. They are usually fundraising, membership drives, etc.

Yuck! You may say this but consider the fact that if you get onto a board for fundraising for the dominant association of the industry you want to have a career, then a few things happen very quickly:

- Access - You suddenly get to meet decision makers and powerful influencers in the industry.
- Exposure - You are able to have good quality time with people who are either drivers in the industry or can introduce you to drivers
- Credibility - You are not just another hat-in-hand job seeker asking to be considered. You are a board member who is working hard to get things done for the industry's top association.

This kind of access and the accompanying earned credibility allows you to meet people in a non-confrontational way (unlike job seeking) where you can be at a peer level instead of superior/subordinate position. You meet, talk and go over things as peers not as superior/subordinate, unlike the interviewing process which invariably is set up to be that way. The association's power brokers, on the other hand, get to know and like you and are able to give you referrals with recommendations for positions that are either going to be posted or are contemplated but not posted!

Helping Hint:
It is best to go meet the member recruitment director of the association to find out if this is the right association to join (for your needs). Attend a mixer so that you know what types of people (position and interests) show up.

Got you interested? Good but hold off on joining until you finish Week 3. There is a good reason to do so but please do the research and attend initial meetings to gauge which association you want to join.

Research Position Paper

This is a very key part of the FTR Career System. It is the critical difference between you and the rest of the market competing and struggling to get past the gatekeepers. I came up with this idea because I realized that resumes (no matter how good they are) are like supermarket or elevator music – all around us, accepted by us, and easily ignored by us.

Please don't misunderstand me, I am not saying that resumes have no value. This is not what I am saying but as the title of the book suggests; the resume should not be the centerpiece of your job finding.

The purpose of the position paper is to show your knowledge and interest in a particular topic and industry instead of submitting a flat one-dimensional resume. You aren't representing that you are an "expert" but rather that you can do research, have a brain, and are eager to pursue the topic or industry. Also the paper's topic should be "hot" or very much on the minds of people in the industry; even controversial.

What does the targeted industry (which you chose) have that is a very HOT topic of the day? What trends or laws yet to be in place are on everyone's lips in the industry. You will know by reading the information on the various industries and what the hottest buzz is. If you aren't sure then type in "what is hot in XYZ industry" in your favorite search engine. Consider a possibly controversial topic that is catching a lot of industry buzz.

Look into the topics and see if one of them is related to what you are interested in.
Examples:

- Security: RFID technology effect on supply chain management and my example
- Video Games: IGA (In game advertising) effectiveness on the video gaming world - Darren's example
- Health providers or Health insurance: HIPAA (Health Insurance Portability and Accountability Act) effect on Insurance and Health Providers in costs and complexities
- Aeropace or Aviation: the industry's impact on carbon footprint and climate change?
- Legal or Marketing: marketing tools for law firms such as RSS, CRMs, etc. - are they helping or hurting the profession?
- Legal: Is legal work outsourcing (say to India) hurting the legal profession?

Get the point? The research paper is about giving a well researched topic a great rendition through your own thinking process. If you are not a good writer, do the research, formulate your conclusions and have a good writer that you know (friend, relative, associate) do a mockup for you.

> *NOTE: The paper does not (will not) need to be perfect and read like Shakespeare. That is perfectly okay. It is the first stab at the process to re-invent and re-tool and so it will not be polished and refined. The refinement comes from more exposure to the industry folks that you will meet, ping and discuss. Reiterate and polish the paper after each meeting.*

PERSONAL CASE CITING:

How I Became an Expert in Something I Didn't Know

When I wrote the first draft on the topic of supply chain security I did a lot of research at the local library (the Library of Congress actually, but hey, I was living in DC at the time) and got a lot of information. But now, you can get a lot of information by combing the internet.

The first efforts were rough but as I spent more interviewing time talking to the people on the original list of 15 targeted companies I got better and more comfortable with the jargon, terms, and concepts used.

It got to the point that in a few interviews people asked me how it is that an industry outsider knew so much about truly leading edge technology? I said they should hire me and find out!

End – Week 2 Actions Review:
Checklist of Accomplishments:

- [x] Identified viable 1 or 2 industry(ies) that you plan to work in
- [x] Identified and researched possible associations that you will be joining to leverage
- [x] Rough draft of position paper (2-3 pages maximum) written

Chapter 9
Week 3 - Research Targets

Start – Week 3 Goals:

You have reached a pivotal week - great going! Now is the time to drill down to the specific companies you will be engaging with!

Checklist:

Necessary tasks to be done:

- ☒ Research 16 firms (within the 1-2 industries you've chosen from Week 2) to figure out what will be your first Top 4 firms to approach.
- ☒ Create folders and information sheets on each of the 16 targeted firms.

Week 3 To Do's:
Research Targeted Firms

This week is solely dedicated to researching the living heck out of the companies within the industry that you want to work for. It starts by creating a short list of the companies that you are eager to pursue – look at a Fortune 500 list for previous years to see which companies fall into what industry classifications. Don't stop there. There are a lot of regional firms that also occupy the industry but are clearly not as big as the Fortune 500 types; please do not write these companies off because there are a LOT of advantages to these firms.

> Most people's natural instincts are to go for the Fortune 500 type companies. Some industries are pretty much dominated by global players (like petrochemical) due to the cost and infrastructure. However, this may not always be the best strategy. Here are reasons why:
>
> **Large and powerful is fine but Fortune 500 types have many disadvantages:**
>
> Too many people going after them – lowers your chances of getting in the door
>
> Many sieve systems to push you out
>
> Snotty attitude with a "dime a dozen" attitude toward new hires
>
> Tend to be non-flexible or accommodating for special situations
>
> **Small firms are fine but:**
>
> Financial strength may not be sustainable (esp. in this economy)
>
> You may not be able to grow or expand to where you want to go due to size constraints
>
> **Medium or regional players may be better because they are big enough to allow you to be employed, grow, and develop without getting lost in the shuffle. Range: $10 million/year to $1 billion/year revenues**

44 • Forget the Resume

If you need to find out who the players are in the industry you picked, remember the industry association research? There should be membership listings of the firms that make up the association.

Research the top 16 companies in the industry (in terms of revenue or market dominance) and get the following information:

- Who are the C suite leaders of the company (CEO, COO, CFO, etc) or the equivalent?
- How big is the firm in revenue and profit?
- What main products and services do they make or offer?
- How big are they in terms of regional or national or global coverage?
- Any information on their developments or participation in the position paper topic you chose for the industry that they are in?
- Can you obtain the email addresses and phone numbers for the C suite folks or the company (if you can't find anything on individuals)?

Helping Hint:
When you find these pages, print a hardcopy and underline whatever strikes you as an interesting fact or noteworthy to remember. Sorry, you can be "green" when you get the job!

Where can you find such information?

Company website –

Look at: **About Us** or **Leadership** or **Governance** sections for information on the leadership

Look at: **Fast Facts** or **Financial** sections for information on the profits and revenues

Look at: **World Map** or **Global Directory** for information on how widespread geographically the company may be

Other sources – the ones that come to mind are:

www.Zoominfo.com

www.LinkedIn.com

www.Wikipedia.org

www.WSJ.com (Wall Street Journal website)

www.Bloomberg.com

Another helpful thing to do is to get on your favorite search engine and type in the company's name, CEO or other leader's name, and/or the position paper's topic. Do a combination of these to see if the internet comes up with anything that may be helpful.

Be very careful when using these various sources as to their accuracy. Even respected sources such as Wall Street Journal or CNN.com have gotten it wrong. When talking to the company employees later put out these factoids as a question such as:

"Is it true that your company's XRT project addresses global warming?"

Create Folders

Make a folder for each company that you have researched. You should now have 16 files for 16 separate companies when you are done with Week 3.

Each folder should be contain the following information pieces:

- Conversation Log Sheet **(See Exhibit 5: Conversation Log Sheet)** – this should be a log of what was done anytime an action relating to this company occurred or to keep track of any conversations as to when (date/time), who were you talking with and what was discussed

- General Information Sheet **(See Exhibit 6: General Information Sheet)** – numbers to call, email addresses, for easy reference – keep in mind that you will be talking to multiple companies and this will come in very handy to keep you professional in response

- Wikipedia Sheet- because they tend to have an amalgam of information sources. It is a great abstract, but carefully check on accuracy as all Wikis are open source and anyone can add or subtract content and there are few if any controls.

- Website information sheet on corporate leaders, divisions/departments, locations, products/services, financial performance info (if available)

- Linked In or Zoominfo sheet on who are possible key players in the firm (limit to 10 or less) and that are in disciplines that you are interested in

- News articles (Bloomberg, Huffington Post, Wall St Journal, The New York Times, and CNN are all possible resources. Be creative.) about company, role of firm in the industry or world, and latest news

 Researching, sifting through, and final selection of who will make up the top 16 firms to be targeted will take the better part of the week. Time to research and assemble all this per file (company) may be 30-40 minutes for initial file setups. As you get more of it done, the learning curve may go down to 15 minutes per file for researching, print outs and setup.

From your readings, determine which firm would fit the appropriate level

- Top 4 – the first 4 firms to go after
- Mid 4 - the second group of 4 firms to pursue
- Low 4 - the third group of 4 firms to pursue
- Alternate 4 – a reserve group of 4 firms to pursue as you cycle through the Top to Low firms

End – Week 3 Actions Review:
Checklist of Accomplishments:

- ☒ Finish your research and pick the Top 4 firms with information folders on 16 firms total
- ☒ Create folder for each targeted firm with information sheets: conversation log, general information and organizational chart
- ☒ Decide which associations to join based on research from Week 2 – don't go broke in the process. If fees to join are in the $100 - $200 range (or less) then it should be purchased. It is an investment in your future.

Chapter 10
Week 4 – Engaging the Targets

Start – Week 4 Goals:

Way to go!! You are on the right track and past the midpoint in this process! By now, you have done a lot of work in order to have reached this week. It is now time for you to have all that work pay off!

Checklist:

Crucial things to get done this week:

- [x] Rehearse the calls you will be making, from opening lines, to possible routes and alternatives for these conversations.
- [x] Target the Top 4 firms' leadership (either CEO or the department head that you are going after) based on your research of the firms
- [x] Role play the call with a friend or family member in order to be able to respond appropriately to the many ways it may go.
- [x] Initiate calls with backup/follow up information

Week 4 To Do's:
The Fearless Method

One of the prongs for getting to the hiring manager is what I called **The Fearless Method**. This is a modification of what I took from Anthony Parinello's *Selling to V.I.T.O* back in Chapter 3 – Desperation = Inspiration.

It involves bypassing the normal sieves and filters that companies put up to talk to the right level person (i.e., hiring manager) by contacting the highest (or one of the highest offices) in the company! I know it sounds crazy but it does work. I doubted it myself when I read *Selling to V.I.T.O.* but it does work if you keep working at it and practice.

Before we get into the mechanics of such a move here's the basis of why you are doing this and the underlying principle behind this action. Specifically, once you get to the CEO's level you will probably NOT talk to the CEO directly and that is totally fine. Who you really want to talk with is the CEO's administrative assistant (secretary) who is the ultimate gatekeeper or alternately someone in the CEO's office if there are multiple administrative assistants. But here's the interesting thing about this particular gatekeeper: She/he keeps the gate for the big boss (the CEO) but not for the other officers of the company such as the other C-band levels (CFO, COO, CIO, etc) or the vice presidents whoever they maybe.

In fact, it has been my experience that assistants are particularly effective at doing two things:

- Directing me to the next band down from the CEO as to the name and level (even their contact information)
- Giving me the ability to invoke her/his name (administrative assistant's name) to open up receptivity on the part of the next rung down

The question is begged: why would this person do this? Well, following human dynamics, most people usually fall into the camp of helpfulness as long as there is no negative repercussions for them to help you. The CEO's administrative assistant is immune from a lot of negative repercussions within the organization as this person is the CEO's right hand when it comes to agenda setting, organizing his/her calendar and impeding or allowing people to approach the throne.

As long as you are asking for guidance to talk to someone lower than her/his boss then the information is usually forthcoming. However, to get an audience with the CEO is another story.

But we don't want to talk to the CEO in this case. Because, as powerful as the CEO may be within the organization, he/she is really not the appropriate person to ask for guidance on the decision maker for hiring people.

The appropriate division or functional silo head is the right person to approach. While I have come across some CEO administrative assistants that do not help the percentage is more like 60-70% that do guide or help.

Usually the CEO's administrative assistant knows very well who the person in Legal Department or the Plastics Division head is. If you have the information already in hand (due to your research) of the head of the division or unit that you want to contact then it helps to lead the call by dropping their name in your request for help

See Exhibit 7: Call Scripts

Why would they do this? Because, once again, there is no negative repercussions to do so. The administrative assistant is the de facto second most powerful person in the company by virtue of the fact of proximity and control of the CEO's world. Would any mere VP dare to challenge them? The answer is "doubtful".

But, this is important, you must get the administrative person's first name. This can be gotten by asking him/her for it and then thanking them. Please see the script.

See Exhibit 7: Call Scripts

 These first calls can be very scary for the following reasons:

- you've never done it before
- it is awkward
- nobody likes cold calls
- it may not work

However, put it into perspective – everything you are doing in the FTR Career System is to get past the normal screening and filtering. Yes, you may be scared at first but with repetition you will get past the fear and, more importantly, get past the screenings!

Remember, the overall goal is to get past the HR and Personnel screens to get to decisionmakers and arrange meetings with them. Get face time using the position paper you wrote from Week 2 so that you establish a positive image of your thinking, interest and abilities!

Helping Hint:

Review the template script section for preparation of the Fearless Method, and do a dry run practice of what you would say in a role play with someone you know. Make the call to the CEO first and if after repeated tries you are blocked time and again then go the next level down the corporate chain which is usually the COO (Chief Operating Officer) or the head of the silo or function where you are seeking a position in.

In order of sequence:

- Call CEO first! Try at least 4-5 times to reach the CEO – see the mechanics of the call in the upcoming section.
- If CEO route does not work, go with the head of silo (VP of HR, Chief Operating Officer, Managing Director for European firms, etc)

(*NOTE: From your research, you should have an idea as to where you are going (say, VP of Business unit X, head of Legal, Chief Information Officer, etc)*)

The Mechanics of the Call

How do you get sent through to the CEO or the head of the silo?

It comes down to decision trees as to how you can approach. Here is an example, most companies have general phone numbers for their headquarters. It usually has a generic block number like:

(206) 555-5400 - as an example

If you call it then you may get a human being or a machine so this is what you do:

See Exhibit 8: Call Progress Decision Tree

Branch 1:

If you get a human being then ask for the office of Mr/Ms. XXXXXX (CEO's name). One scenario is that you are immediately sent through to the CEO's office. Follow the Fearless Method script. When the administrative assistant gives you the name of that person (say, the head of Plastics division) then ask for the CEO's administrative assistant's name and use it to thank him/her (like " thank you so much Nancy") then ask if she can transfer you through to the head of Plastics division. If not, then hang up and call back to the general line and ask for the head of Plastics division.

Branch 1a:

If you get a human being but they ask you what it is about (screening) then follow the Fearless Method script regarding the topic of your position paper. If they ask for more clarification or shunt you off to having you call or email a flunky department then thank them and hang up. See Branch 3.

Branch 2:

If you get a machine then it will ask you to type in or say your intended person's name (usually last name first). Type it in. Now it may get you to the CEO's office then follow the Fearless Method script.

Branch 2a:

If you get a machine but it says it is a blocked line then hang up. See Branch 3.

Branch 3:

It is at this time that you look at trying variations of the phone number block sequence such as example given (206) 555 5400 then dial up (206) 555-5414 or 5478 or 5402. Play with the number sequence. Most of the time you will still be calling the same company but different individuals in the company.

When you get someone live (because these are the number sequence that have real people attached to them) then ask to be sent to CEO's office following Branch 1 or Branch 1a scenarios. Start off by saying "Hi, I am sorry but I've been bounced around a bit in my call to Mr. XXXXX (CEO) so could you please help to send me through to his/her office?"

If that person sends you through to the CEO, follow Fearless Method script for CEO admin.

If that person does not transfer you, thank them and hang up.

(NOTE: If you try 4-5 times using the random dialing and it proves fruitless, go to Branch 4.)

Branch 4:

Okay, at this stage the CEO is solidly insulated from the real world! Try the next level down whether that be the COO or CFO (Chief Financial Officer) or the Senior Vice President or the head of the silo you want (Legal, HR, Compliance) or the division you want (Plastics, Turbines, Engineering). Repeat the process starting from Branch 1.

✓ This is the not-so-fun part of the process but you are only doing this one company at a time and only for the Top 4 companies you have targeted (for now).

✓ Of the many scores of companies I have done this for – not only for getting a job but for getting face time with decision makers in the field of sales – there has only been ONE TIME that this method was totally stymied and I got nowhere. One time out of 30+ times.

Personal Case Citing:

Aim High and Shoot High and Get Results

Besides job hunting (Chapter 3 Desperation = Inspiration), I have used the Fearless Method for:

- Getting meeting time with major companies during my sales efforts. Companies such as:
    - American Express
    - Sysco Foods
    - ExxonMobil
    - Coca Cola Company
    - UPS
    - Georgia Pacific
    - Honeywell

- Resolving personal business matters (bills that don't make sense or have charges that aren't correct):
    - Allstate Insurance (policy glitch resolved in two hrs)
    - Delta Airlines (nonrefundable tickets refunded in 1 week)
    - Bank of America (3 erroneous late payments that were corrected in 4.5 hrs)

I am telling you this not to brag but to demonstrate to you that this is a very, very effective tool to get things done very quickly from on high.

Helping Hints:

Chase down all Top 4 targets till you get results – if you reach a dead end after repeated tries (this Week 4 then Week 5 then Week 6, drop the target). The next target in Mid 4 list – moves up for every Top 4 target that is dropped. The other way a Top 4 target drops from the list of calls is if you get through and are engaged with a possible hiring manager.

You should get at least 1-2 Top 4 targets engaged by either meeting or sending the position paper which should help you to meet with the company managers.

Establishing Personal "Champions"

So once you get the head of the Plastics division and he/she sends you down to their director of PVC piping to discuss the hottest trend in plastics of amalgams (made up purely for illustrative purposes) now what?

What you are doing is to co-opt the person you are meeting to be on your side. To help you along the way, you need someone inside who believes you have potential to work with them and to help "champion" you to his/her peers. This person can be invaluable to give you the real story of the company, possible postings, and possible pitfalls or political landmines that you should avoid. It helps to be humble but confident. It may be a game of waiting or deflection where he/she sends you to another associate that you will meet and (hopefully) impress.

Helping Hint:
Always, always, always send a thank you note to the person(s) you talked to for the first time. Once again, notes should be handwritten and legible with a quick (short) but sincere thank you for his/her time.

Helping Hint:
Follow up intermittently (maybe 2 week intervals) if it is a waiting game. A prompting email or phone call keeps you fresh on their mind.

BEGINNER NOTES:

Like a term paper, you must take the information you got from meetings regarding your topical position paper and, after verifying with fact checking, incorporate into your paper to make it more robust. Be careful not to give out industrial secrets if the information that was given to you by a company employee. How would you know this happened? The information is nowhere to be found on internet relating to the company. Refine and hone your paper to give it more detail and relevance.

Remember, the stated reason for the meetings is to talk about the company's interest in the hot topic or trend of the position paper. However, as you ask well placed questions in order to raise your profile and position yourself as a possible new and immediately beneficial employee. These questions could be along the lines of the following, if we are talking about piping a shown in the example:

"How do you see your company taking amalgams to the next level in terms of use and applicability?"

"Why did amalgams suddenly become of great interest to the plastics world?"

"What do you think are some shortcomings of amalgam?"

The funny thing is that the more pithy questions you ask (and take notes on), the more you come across as being smart and sharp. Also, you are NOT being interviewed but are actually interviewing them.

Ask questions toward end of meeting (about 2/3 into the meeting time) about possibilities of positions opening up on a fulltime basis. Or ask what type of employees they are seeking in terms of background and education, but also experience that is needed. Broach, a little bit, the fact that you have these skills and traits.

> ✓ Obviously you can't keep on asking questions throughout the whole time (and you wouldn't want to either). Looking at your notes (that you carried with you to the meeting) drop hints of your knowledge and homework done on the company throughout the conversation.
>
> It is best to do this in the form of a question such as
>
> > "Is it true that your company's XRJ 6000 project is the most advanced state of amalgams?"
> >
> > "Is the breakdown rate of the amalgams usually within 5-9%?"
>
> Why a question? Because if you state the factoid that you read from the internet or Wikipedia and it is wrong then you won't look like a pompous fool if you ask it in the form of a question. It's called fact checking and it impresses.

Reality CHECK

End – Week 4 Actions Review:
Checklist of Accomplishments:

- [x] Understand Fearless Method technique and practice it with a friend or family member
- [x] Research best numbers to use to contact CEO or department head
- [x] Call the numbers to get to targeted person in target company
- [x] Chase down all targeted companies and pursue until you have definitely hit a dead end – no progress, simply blocked, no call backs or emails, no invitation to move forward, etc.

Chapter 10: Engaging the Targets

Chapter 11
Week 5 – Multiple Targets Engaged

Okay, here is an "Atta Boy" or "Atta Girl" for being focused and sticking with the program!! Great, great job thus far!! You should be proud that you've gotten so far in such a short time! Give yourself a pat on the back!

Now is when it gets fun and interesting!!

Start – Week 5 Goals:
Checklist:

Build up on what you've done in Week 4 by:

- Continue to follow up on Top 4 targets
- Go onto Mid 4 targets on a rolling list basis
- Make notes and set appointments for interview or information interview
- Continue to refine position paper through research and readings
- Go to association meetings to find 3 types of people

Week 5 To Do's:
Professionally Pursued Targets

I am not a life coach. Never have been and never will be. What comes next is a discipline that you must impose on yourself for 3-4 months or as long as it takes to get you to the job/career that you want for yourself! Stay focused and be your own life coach!

Here are some-stay-focused points:

- Make phone calls and follow up on the targeted companies starting with the Top 4 firms. Concentrate on them solely in Weeks 4 and 5!

- Best times to call: in the morning (8 am – 8:30 am), right before lunch (11:30-12:30p) and at end of day (even after hours – 5:30 to 6:30 pm) in no particular order because everyone is different. Why those times? Less gatekeepers and more likelihood that you will get through to the person that you need to connect with as most hiring managers are operational and work early and late hours. (If they hire you, maybe their load will be lessened!) Also, mix it up for the people you called in terms of the timeframes you have tried to get hold of them (you can track this by writing in your Conversation Log Sheet when you called and either left a message or not).

 Helping Hint:
It is best to leave 1 week blocks of time for someone to get back to you if you leave a message because they can be very busy or traveling or both. It is not smart to leave a trail of voicemails in a week every time you get the person's phone.

> **Helping Hint:**
> This is where the administrative assistant of the person you are talking to is INVALUABLE!!! Ask him/her when the manager is available or best time to reach the target contact.
>
> Ask the admin for his/her mobile number. You may or may not receive it. I've asked for it and gotten it many times only because I asked in a confident voice.

- Get on a schedule and take two 15 minute breaks because the intensity of the efforts in calling people and getting shot down or deflected is TOUGH. However, you will get past the initial fear and move forward to making this a regular thing.

- For people calling you back please remember to answer phone respectfully and professionally especially if your caller ID number is "Unknown". First impressions, especially over the phone where there are no visual "cues" are critical. If you are at your home office then have the General Information and Conversation Log Sheet handy so that you can talk to the return caller and write down notes or schedule things right there and then.

- The point of discussion isn't about you or what you can do but to know more about the company's interest in the new hot topic or trend (position paper's topic). Meeting them about this is the goal for the interviews!

(*NOTE: This then takes the conversation AWAY from being about employment which most managers react by punting you over to the HR or personnel departments. It is a safe environment to talk about a topic/project that they are deeply interested in (as you are too).*)

> **Helping Hint:**
> After you hang up from the phone call then put that person's name, title, company and phone number and email in the contact section of your smartphone (if you have one) This enables you to identify them immediately if they call again.

> **Helping Hint:**
> It is best to call on your landline (if you have one) for outgoing calls because the phone reception is usually better and the likelihood of dropped call incidences is much lower. Leave your mobile number for callbacks because you are more likely to have the phone on if you need to be away from your home office.

56 • Forget the Resume

- Remember to be tenacious but not irritating. It is not easy. I tend to be too tenacious in going after a target. The point is to meet and the ways for that are:
    1. Calls to get people's okay to send info or to meet
    2. Send position paper if they are not willing to meet and follow up with phone call once sent (about a week)

(*NOTE: DO NOT SEND a resume but if it is requested to provide one, tell them that you would rather send the topical position paper. Have the person look at your position paper FIRST!!! Resumes can be given when you meet them. AND, NO, YOU ARE NOT BLOWING YOUR CHANCE TO GET A JOB THIS WAY!!*)

- Top 4 targets are fulfilled (taken off the call list) when one of two things occur:
    1. Total and utter rejection from all the contact points you are trying to reach – via CEO or head of the silo and their subordinates. Very unlikely.
    2. Getting onto a real good job lead with influencers or decision makers which gives you access to strong lead into a position or post

This process allows you to roll up Mid 4 targets to concentrate on them one at a time. The system uses a rolling list format (when one is taken off the list then the next lower one takes its place).

✓ Remember the goal is to limit your targets to approximately 16 firms (counting the alternates) and get job offers from 2-3 of them!

✓ Anticipate that you will be deflected, delayed, shunted off, or shot down initially when you work on your Top 4 target companies because you will be unsure of yourself and the steps you need to take. The process of engaging people will teach you how to navigate and get through to the right persons.

✓ Be honest and forthright. Some people will be jerks to you because they don't care about you or they are just plain rude because they were raised by mole rats! Please get past them, take the higher ground and be as professional and warm as you can be! A nice Southern lady used to tell me, "kill them with kindness." This usually works very well.

Leveraging Association Power!

Go to association meetings (not just mixers) and work to get on a board or committee. Volunteer for jobs like fundraising or membership committees - why? Because nobody likes to do stuff like that and so there tend to be vacancies in those committees. These are blessings in disguise because in the process of doing these tasks you are meeting and forming connections with a lot of association members under the banner of the association's work and not because you are trying to "network" with them.

You may think this is distractive and extra work that you don't need for job finding but it helps on two important fronts:

1. Get In Front of Personal Champions!

Gets you in front of people (some influencers, some connectors and some decision makers)

Enables you to meet with industry folks which you need to know when you get the job in the industry you have targeted. The goal is to meet 3 types of people:

1. **Influencers** – people who can't hire you in the company or organization that they are in but are very influential in pointing you to or, even better, introducing you to the right people who can hire you in their organizations (ie, Personal Champion)
2. **Connectors** – borrowing a page from Malcolm Gladwell's *Tipping Point* – these are people who know a lot of people and are living/breathing Rolodexes of people connectors. As an example: On Linked In, people with 500+ connections.
3. **Decision makers** – the ones who can and are able to hire you

Approach influencers and connectors with confidence AND humility and ask them for help.

The opening lines such as:

"Kathy, I seek your guidance on…"

"Jim, I was wondering if you could tell me…"

"Antonia, what do you think about…"

Just that simple. When I need someone's help I say "I need your guidance and help. I am probably not going to be able to reciprocate right away but I really do appreciate whatever help you can offer to get me to the right hiring manager or person who can further guide me."

(NOTE: I don't ask to speak to a department or HR - NEVER!! This is the big black hole from whence you will never emerge!)

2. Be a Knowledge Mover in the Industry

What is a "knowledge mover"? A knowledge mover is someone who know his/her stuff from the industry by absorbing intelligence, data, and information from the people that inhabit the industry and then moving forward to improve the industry he/she is in. Those improvements could range from accurately communicating the industry's goals and vision to the outside world improving industry alignment internally, or bringing your own innovation or technology to the industry!

You can be dialed into leading edge information just by mere virtue of proximity. This makes you more valuable to industry folks who (if they see you doing really good and cool things) will take notice and approach you for who-knows-what! Usually good stuff though.

 In the association venue, you don't need to talk about the topic of the position paper but don't seem overly pushy or anxious about getting a job either! The trick is to seem interested in the firms but not desperate or clinging! Nothing is more irritating than a clingy person! Relax and have fun while you make it fun! Question: which would you rather want to hang around? A nervous Chihuahua like person who always wants to impress you with his/her knowledge and accomplishments OR a person who listens, engages you, and is funny and keeps it light but gets serious when necessary? That's what perceptions may be like for you so keep it in mind.

End – Week 5 Actions Review:
Checklist of Accomplishments:

- ☒ Make more calls to get to decisionmakers from the Top 4 target list.
- ☒ Make calls to Mid 4 target list as Top 4 targets are eliminated either by total rejection or getting a strong lead on the decision makers
- ☒ Attend association meetings and push for getting on a board or committee

Chapter 12
Week 6 – Interviewing Process

Congratulations!!! You are beginning to hit your stride, the process should be more natural now and now you can really start working those connections. Did I say last week was the fun part? This is the fun part – engaging to get the job or position of your desire! The title of this chapter is misleading. With the FTR Career System you are actually interviewing the company's hiring manager and not the other way around!

Start – Week 6 Goals:

- Continue with the calls for Top 4 and Mid 4 targets
- Develop more file information on Low 4 targets (companies and people there)
- Continue with meetings with associations – carry out tasks and functions that may be assigned
- Begin interviews with targeted company personnel with the goal of talking about the firm and the topic of the position paper (NOT getting a job)!

Week 6 To Do's:

The following is the FTR Career System's Interview Road Map which is for your usage on what to do and why you are doing it during the meeting/interview with the targeted company's people. However, in this process (unlike a typical job interviewing session) you are not the interviewee as much as the interviewer! Why? Because you are not interviewing for a job but rather talking about the industry topic that your position paper addressed.

The Physical Stuff:
Location:

The physical address is something that you need to make sure that you have a good handle on. Let me explain. Being a professional salesperson I have gone to many, many appointments throughout the US and the world and I have the following rules of thumb:

- When you get the physical address from the person you're going to meet ask if it is pretty straight forward to find the office. This is because some offices have entrances that are not at the front of the building but need to be accessed in other ways. The last thing you want here is to be late because you couldn't find the front door!

- When you receive the address showing the location and directions via GPS or some mapping algorithm, make super sure you know how to get there and the traffic patterns (rush hour traffic, worker construction, road repair) are factored in. Treat the appointment as if going on a plane – give yourself a fudge factor of 1 hr. DON'T BE LATE!!!

 I've interviewed many applicants in my life and only one actually got hired even though he was late – the rest weren't even considered.

BEGINNER NOTES:

Murphy's Law always kicks in when you go to these things – spilled coffee, traffic jams, etc. So, don't drink any beverages on the way to the meeting and allow PLENTY of extra time because if you don't then you will lose out!

Timeframe:

Make sure that you and the company manager set a date and time and day and location clearly. Confirm in an email so that there is NO question or doubt as to what that day/time/location really is. If the appointment is more than a week away, send an email the day before the appointment confirming for the following day.

If the location is one you have to fly to, then make sure that you account for time zone differences!

 ### Helping Hint

If you are running late because something crazy happened then text or call your appointment as soon as you know that you are not able to make it on time. It is always better to show up early and not be distracted, nervous and upset because you were late or cut it too close!

Attire:

Dress appropriate to the company's typical attire or dress code – if the company is a startup and everyone is casual then for men please wear nice shirt and slacks (business casual). If the company is old school like financial companies or banks then dress professionally with suit, tie, etc.

If you are unsure then dress up with suit and tie. You can always take off the tie and suit if you are wrong!

  Not to be annoying or sound like your parent, but nose rings, earrings, flowers, hats, etc that reflect your true free spirit and individuality needs to be left at home. Trust me on this one!

> **Helping Hint:**
> Keep your suit rolled up neatly while traveling to the appointment so that there are no ugly wrinkles all over and it doesn't look like you slept in the suit. Look crisp, clean and sharp! Europeans usually don't have an issue with wrinkly clothing as much as Americans but play it on the safe side.

Hygiene:

(I'll keep this short and to the point):

Hair (on the head or on the face): Keep it trimmed and cleaned. No "greasy" look please.

Mouth: Brush and use mouthwash. NO garlic laced sandwiches please! NO, I repeat, NO food items like spinach!!!!! No coffees or teas or soft drinks – they can spill onto you very easily.

Clothing: All buttons buttoned, all zippers zipped – I think you know what I mean

Vision wear: If you normally wear glasses but you have contacts it is best to go in with glasses because if you have issues with contacts then that might distract you from the meeting

What you need with you:

- [x] Pen that writes well
- [x] Pad of paper
- [x] Your calling cards (10 pack)
- [x] Copies of position paper in a nice binder – 5 sets
- [x] Copies of resume in the same binder – 5 sets
- [x] Cash
- [x] Debit/credit card
- [x] Phone – switch to mute/off before going to meeting – please remember to do this!
- [x] Company's file where you have made notes and researched the specifics for this meeting

All of this to be carried in a nice professional folio or brief

The Mental Stuff:

These are the 3 things you must accomplish during the meetings:

1. Intelligence Gathering:

You must do your homework on the company and possibly the person that you are interviewing (the appointment) via Linked In

Use the templated questions (**See Exhibit 9: Template Baseline Questions**) working from outside to in. Asking questions pertaining to the company, the topic and the person's opinion on both subjects

Goals of the interview are:

- Get more information on the company and the division that you are interested in such as:
    1. Structure and locations of the division
    2. People who are in charge and populate management
    3. Challenges and positives to the division and the company
- Attain more information on the trend or hot topic (of your position paper):
    1. How does this impact the industry or company?
    2. What type of progress has the company made on this trend, if any?
    3. How does this trend open up job prospects either fulltime or contractor?
- Interviewee's personal impressions of:
    1. Where trend is taking the industry?
    2. Are there other trends that impact industry? Anything else that the company is promoting?
    3. What kind of people does he/she think are needed to address this new type of trend or work in the company?

(NOTE: You are shepherding the conversation from out to in (ever tightening circles) - in terms of going from industry and company information to trend/topic info to interviewee's impressions information. This is key because he/she may give a good picture of prospects within the company.)

All this is to hone the conversation in on the next step…

- Your possible "fit" into the company:
    1. What does it take to join the company?
    2. What are some ways to get started on the process?
    3. Are there any projects that are being thought of or contemplated that might have a need for people like you?
    4. Introduce your position paper and ask them to read and critique for you – deem it a high honor
    5. DO NOT LEAVE THE RESUME if you are NOT asked for it!!!! That will be for later. Let him/her concentrate on the position paper!
    6. Ask him/her if there is anyone else in the firm you could talk to on this topic
    7. Introduce the idea that you will call him/her in about a week or week and a half for initial impressions on the paper. Hopefully, he/she has positive impressions about more than just your research paper but that is for later.

Helping Hint:

DON'T RELY ON MEMORY!!!!!!! Write down in bullet form the things that he/she is saying to you. This will be used for your notes on the company and to refine the position paper. Write observational notes on the person as well (hobbies, vacations, spouse, kids, etc) The peculiar nature of asking good and thoughtful questions is that you come across a whole lot smarter than you would if you made statements of knowledge or about yourself

✓ Don't ask questions just to ask questions – you know the kind I mean. "Duh" questions that can easily be answered if you looked at the corporate website or can be obtained from an elementary or peripheral internet search. You want to impress this person.

2. Inject Your Thoughts and Observations

- Inform the discussion with injection of information that you have gotten from your research on the industry, company and/or the topic – but do it smartly. Don't say "I know that X is a very important part of your company" but rather say it this way "My understanding is that X is a very important part of your company, is that true?" If so then ask "why?"

- Once again it is NOT about you but do inject at appropriate times your thoughts and insights. Do it in the form of questions (like Jeopardy game show style) that requires validation. Why? Because if you are wrong or if the person does not agree with you then you won't come across as a know-it-all show off.

- Feedback is key! Ask them what they think of your thoughts (Example: "Is my understanding correct on this?" or "Do you think that I might be a good fit in the company/division?")

PERSONAL CASE CITING:

Nothing New Under the Sun

When I was going through the interview meetings for the position in DC, I met the person that I sent the position paper. When I asked the hiring manager what he thought about my position paper he said "Look, it's a pretty good paper but you're not telling me anything that I don't already know."

I replied that it was not my intent to tell him something that was new to him but that I wanted to know if my thinking and analysis was tracking along the lines that the company was moving toward.

It was then that he enthusiastically said "Yes" and proceeded to give me more ideas to pursue and people to talk to!

*Note: IN CASE YOU MISSED IT THE FIRST 10 TIMES: If they ask you for the resume, you **must** give them the position paper!! **Don't leave them with just the resume!!!!** I can't stress this enough.*

3. Map out Next Steps:

- When the meeting time allotted is near the end and you see that he/she is getting antsy then start to wind it down.
- You don't need to make a defining statement of why you would be good in this firm.
- Simply ask him/her what are the next possible routes to take to pursue a possible fit within the company or project team for you. Listen and write down what he/she says. If you are unclear or not sure of what they are saying, ask for more clarification.

Note: Did you notice that the conversation shifted from the company, the paper, etc to you?

No one is "fooled" by the basic premise of why you are there. You haven't gone in there to do a term paper; the manager sitting across from you knows that. But it is the WAY you went about getting information about possible "fit" with the company that makes solicitation of this information so non-threatening!

- Do ask for help in pushing this initiative forward with follow up either with him/her later or someone else in a reasonable timeframe (say, 1-2 weeks from now).
- Thank them for their time and guidance! This is crucial. Leave them with a very positive image and feel for you!

After Action Steps

- Take notes and summarize the outcomes on the conversation log with date/time/location information. Write this down as soon as possible after you have cleared the area from your meeting while the information is still fresh in your mind.
- Schedule a forward tickler notice as to when to call him/her in a week or week and a half
- Send a handwritten (legible) note of thanks to the person you met and mail the next day
- Refine the position paper with the information that you gleaned from the interview (be careful not to include any proprietary information into the paper that may have been accidentally shared with you by the interviewee)

End – Week 6 Actions Review:
Checklist of Accomplishments:

- ☒ Continue to approach and process the Top 4, Mid 4, Low 4 targets
- ☒ Set up meetings for informational interviews about the topic you wrote the position paper on
- ☒ Go to meetings of targeted associations and work to get on a board or committee

> ✓ The point is to infiltrate the targeted companies (targeted 16 firms) as far and as deep as possible. Introducing yourself and meeting as many people within that firm is key. (Getting sticky with the organization)
>
> ✓ Resist the temptation and natural tendency to be too "familiar" or get cocky with talking to the company's employees. This is the fastest way for the door to be shut in your face no matter how cool they thought you were initially.

Reality CHECK

Chapter 13
Look Back

A quick review of what the FTR Career System's multi-pronged approach should net you:

Homework:

Having completed all the steps then you will be very well equipped to engage with the people that you meet at the targeted firms.

More meetings = better and refined information! This information not only goes into the position paper but is in your notes and brain to pull out and use during the meetings. Remember, you are not required to be an expert but someone who is pursuing more information to be fairly knowledgeable.

Fearless Method:

Engaging with the hiring managers by cold calling to the top and asking to talk to the next level down is important to cut through all the massive filters, sieves and red tape that naturally surround a company. It seems the bigger the company the more BS you have to cut through! The position paper is key device to show them how you think, organize your thoughts and convey them to others!

Once you begin meeting company personnel here are the things that need to be done:

- Meet and get as deep and sticky with the targeted firm's personnel as you can
- Get as much information on the industry, company, and topic/trend as you can during the meetings
- Move the ball forward in ferreting out if there are projects, tasks or positions that are opening up or just being contemplated and go after the key decision makers to consider you as strong candidate – this can be done by referrals of the people you have already interviewed or by connector references or by association references (see below)

This process may take some time to sift out all 16 targets (Top 12 + 4 alternates) – from 3-6 months but the process will naturally accelerate and heat up as you master the learning curve of your own FTR Career System.

 **Helping Hint:**
follow up with the interviewees and find out:

- *His/her thought on the paper? Areas for improvement or change?*
- *Who else can you talk to about this topic in the company?*
- *Upcoming or current positions contemplated or posted?*
- *Company's stance on the topic or trend?*
- *Upcoming or current projects that are contemplated?*

✓ Please be extremely careful NOT to divulge proprietary information given to you (by accident) in the interviews. How do you know if certain information is proprietary? Look it up under Google and the company's name. No mention? Then it is probably proprietary.

Association Leverage:

Joining boards or committees to help them in their work such as membership drives or fundraising is a great way to get in and get pivotal spots where you are able to meet and touch industry leaders (and their subordinates).

At these meetings work to see what Personal Champions you can develop in 3 types of people:

- Influencers who can point and guide you to people that they know and who are able to sway decision makers
- Connectors who can "connect" you to people who would further pull you to other possible opportunities
- Decision makers who are the people who can hire you (or be part of a selection committee to hire)

 Helping Hint:
Possibly leverage your association knowledge to be introduced to people in the targeted firms to talk and meet about topic/trend or positions or projects that are upcoming

Connectors:

Whether you meet them at a speaking engagement, cocktail party, association board meeting or Fearless Method interview, these people are priceless because they can really broaden AND deepen your search to areas where you may not even know exist (industry sub sectors or companies).

These people usually are LinkedIn folks with 300 - 500+ connections and have been in their industry for a long time! The best way to approach is with confidence but humility as well. Don't be afraid to ask for guidance and help but in a REAL way, that is, so that the connector would call someone on your behalf (or email) instead of you are just given a name and number to call with no participation by the connector. Try to see if you can get multiple names (4-5 references) per connector whenever possible.

Personal Case Citing:

Drilling Down 'til you Find Oil!

If you recall, my DC job search and acquisition project had me engage with 15 firms of which I had 8 of them dialoguing with me for multiple times with various hiring managers. The net result was 2 job offers in 4 months! Your results may vary (as the commercials are wont to say) but you will find your 16 firms will take you further and deeper than you could have by throwing-it-against-the-wall-and-see if-it-sticks approach!

I have heard some folks sending out 200-300+ resumes out into the ether (job postings, Craigslist, want ads, corporate website job application pages) and come up with a big fat ZERO!

The time and energy spent to do that is horrendous and it is very hard work! And, bottom line, do you get what you really want at the end of the day?

Chapter 14
Look Forward

Congratulations!! You should be rightfully proud of yourself to have persevered through a very intensive 6 weeks. Looking back you can see how the progression of work has led you to working with potential employers but in a vastly different fashion than the hat-in-hand form of job searches that most people are doing.

Now that you have completed the Forget the Resume Career System you really have no excuse for not putting it into motion. The job you want is out there if you want it. If you don't then you won't. It is just as simple as that.

There is a very large community of people searching for the right job with the right company so that they can work till retirement. They may be employed, underemployed, or unemployed. They are not there yet but they are striving to be. I am reminded time and again of how big that community really is when the subject of jobs and job satisfaction comes up. It is good to speak with people in these groups to get a sense and a form of comfort that you are not alone.

However, you now have the tools to transition to a level that allows you to chart your own course so that if any other bumps in the road occur then you are empowered to take on the challenge instead of fearing it! Remember desperation = inspiration but more importantly, with the right tools in hand, they can help you move to where you need to go. Life is never easy but we tend to make it harder than it should be by all the messages of negativity and ignorance and doing the same things over and over again expecting a radical change. It is always disappointing when no change comes.

There is a VERY BIG WORLD out there! Beyond your town, city, state and national boundaries. Let the road of life take you wherever it goes and change/iterate with it instead of shrinking from it or running in the opposite direction. Speaking from my personal experience, it is the only attitude to have in life!

Stay on course. If you have any questions post them on my blog at www.Forgettheresume.com. To the degree I can help, I will do so.

Good luck and God speed!

Exhibits

Exhibit 1 73
John Lee's Position Papers (Chapter 3)
    Version 1: Unisys
    Version 2: Pinkerton
    Version 3: Pinkerton

Exhibit 2 81
The Serious Job Finder's Schedule – Darren's Version (Chapter 5)

Exhibit 3 82
Darren's Position Paper Version 3 (Chapter 5)

Exhibit 4 89
The Serious Job Finder's Schedule – Blanks with Notes (Chapter 7)

Exhibit 5 96
Conversation Log Sheet - Sample (Chapter 9)
Conversation Log Sheet - Blank (Chapter 9)

Exhibit 6 98
General Information Sheet - Sample (Chapter 9)
General Information Sheet - Blank (Chapter 9)

Exhibit 7 100
Call Scripts (Chapter 10)

Exhibit 8 104
Call Progress Tree (Chapter 11)

Exhibit 9 105
Template Baseline Questions (Chapter 12)

Exhibit 10 106
Recommended Reading List

EXHIBIT 1

John Lee's Position Papers:
Version 1: Unisys

Supply Chain Management Security Brief

"It was the best of times, it was the worst of times… …" Charles Dickens

INTRODUCTION

After 9/11/01 it seems that everyone (the military, government agencies, private industry) are scrambling to make sense of one question:

> How do we protect the people, cargo, and infrastructure of the United States?

The question opens up a very large opportunity for Unisys to explore because the need for security is no longer that of protection from terrorism but also from the more mundane (yet equally costly) crimes of: smuggling contraband, counterfeit goods, thievery, hijacking, etc. These costs have been estimated at $50 billion per annum in the U.S.

SITUATION

The question pre-dates 9/11 in the supply chain world but the tragedy has brought it to the forefront as to the pervasive weaknesses of a very efficient but porous transportation network.

Consider the following:

- Approximately 90 percent of the world's cargo moves by container.
- Globally, over 48 million full cargo containers move between major seaports each year
- Since 1995, trade volume moving through the nation's 102 seaports has nearly doubled.
- In 2001, U.S. Customs processed more than 214,000 vessels and 5.7 million sea containers.
- Only 2% of the approximately 5.7 million containers that pass through the US are inspected each year. With only 30% of those containing material that matches the cargo manifest.
- 16 million+ containers arrive in the US by ship, truck, and rail. US Customs processed 25 million entries in 2001.

EXHIBIT 1 (CONT'D)

PROBLEM (in implementing solutions):

As illustrated, the scope is staggering. There are dynamics that further complicate matters:

1. The patchwork of legislation and initiatives (sometimes contradictory) that has produced this list of legislation related to homeland security:

    - USA Patriot Act
    - Trade Act of 2002
    - Enhanced Border Security and Visa Reform Act
    - Aviation and Transportation Security Act of 2001
    - Homeland Security Act of 2002
    - Maritime Transportation Security Act of 2002
    - Data Management Improvement Act (DMIA)
    - Bioterrorism Act of 2002

    Other fragments of security solutions:

    - Operation Safe Commerce (OSC)
    - Container Security Initiative (CSI)
    - Free and Secure Trade Program (FAST)
    - Smart and Secure Travel Lanes (SSTL)
    - Sea Cargo Targeting Initiative
    - TWIC
    - Electronic Supply Chain Manifest System
    - US Canada Smart Border Action Plan
    - Customs Trade Partnership Against Terrorism (C-TPAT)
    - International Trade Data System (ITDS)

2. Who's in charge – the U.S. Coast Guard, Transportation Security Administration, or Bureau of Customs and Border Protection or any of the 22 agencies under the Department of Homeland Security? This creates administrative disconnects such as the Coast Guard essentially running ports, ships and inspections (not their historic core competencies) and TSA having cargo authority? How would that be parsed out and who is doing what? No one knows for sure as infighting and territorialism has taken hold of some of the agencies' relationships.

3. Private sector and local (port) authorities are taking their own initiatives. Wal-Mart is working with their vendors on RF tagging their freight movements and are expecting full deployment within 2 years. New York/New Jersey are working on financing (through bond issues) the ability to create their own homeland security programs. Others are starting to fall suit as they realize that the federal government may rely more on "stick" than "carrot" in the implementation of homeland security initiatives.

APPROACH TO SOLUTIONS:

So what does this all mean for Unisys? Simply put: <u>opportunity</u>.

The opportunity to use the combined acumen of Unisys depth of experience as an integrator, consultant, and transportation/security expert.

The approach needs to include the following:

> **Multi-market approach.** To look only for federal money in the classic DOD contracting format will not suffice for "securitizing" ports/ships/rail/air/facilities. That is only one facet and most probably not the largest section. Rather emphasis should also be on state, port and private sector initiatives.
>
> **Cost/liability reduction motives.** To activate port and private sector interest in adopting expensive security measures means that we must show them very tangible benefits from such measures.
>
> A way to justify increasing security tools is to show the offsetting savings of dramatic reduction in pilferage, hijacking, and smuggling. Consider this:
>
> 88% of thefts were of cargo in trailers/containers parked by the side of the road or in lots
> 7% of thefts were burglaries in warehouses
> 5% of thefts were from hijackings
>
> **The average loss per incident is $187,000 in 2002**
>
> **Expertise.** What people (whether they be in government or private industry) are looking for is somebody that can make their lives easier by taking away the threat, hassles, and risks attendant to their responsibility. Unisys needs to position itself as the domain expert that will make this happen.

APPLICATION

In order to implement with the least amount of time and the most amount of efficacy, the company will need to have a liaison that will make the connective bridge between Unisys domain expertise and the port, government, transportation, and logistics sectors. **I would like to render my service to that mission.**

Using my background in designing, planning, selling and executing <u>total supply chain management (SCM)</u> packages for companies such as: Weyerhaeuser, Starbucks, Keytronic, Boise Cascade, Genie Industries, Safeway, Pepsico, etc., I am able to understand the infrastructure, dynamics and successful packaging of systems/products to the transportation industry.

With my history of business development and project team management, I am able to identify targets, move the transaction along quickly and guide it to successful completion.

SUMMARY

Unisys has a wonderful opportunity in serving this country (as well as others) and capturing a very large piece of the homeland security endeavor. Time, expertise and access is very important at this critical juncture. That is why it is imperative that this opportunity to solve a very major headache in the transportation industry is not lost forever.

It is with this in mind that I would like to be considered for a position with Unisys to develop business for its suite of security solutions.

I can be reached at _____

EXHIBIT 1 (CONT'D)

John Lee's Position Papers:
Version 2: Pinkerton

White Paper on Pinkerton Business Development Potential

This world is changing rapidly especially in terms of new areas of revenue generation. Security issues are inextricably bound to accountability and better inventorying for firms and that translates to a better return on investment (ROI). Here are some macro factors that are driving the markets and individual companies:

Real Issues Confronting the Markets:

1. **Private Sector:** Walmart and Target are both mandating that their top 100 vendors will have EPC (electronic product coding) at the case and pallet level to increase security and asset visibility. This will entail active and passive RFID (radio frequency ID) tagging as part of its measure. This will be done by early January 2005. The rest of their vendors must have EPC and RFIDs done by end of 2006. This translates to approximately 1.3 billion cartons that will be converted. The profit potential is staggering for those able to deploy this program effectively.

2. **Government Sector:** Commissioner Robert Bonner of U.S. Customs and Border Protection has stated his agency's intent to create a "green lane" for CT-PAT shippers that will involve "smart containers" with better seals and processes in place. These shippers will enjoy fast entry and exit out of ports via a "green lane".

3. **Global Realities:** As more offshoring of suppliers and vendors are done by Western (U.S. and European) firms to countries with lower cost of production but newer and better machinery (such as in mainland China) the purchase price variances (PPV) becomes a huge reason for companies to maintain the level of savings. These savings are eroded by pilferage, piracy, counterfeiting, and supply chain inefficiencies (redundancies) as a result of poor security, planning and accountability.

So what does that mean to the management of a company? What keeps them up at night? Here are the top "driver" issues that I have come across.

Real Issues Confronting Executive Teams:

1. **The need to increase productivity by greater visibility** using tracking and tracing devices appropriate to the cargo type. More expensive cargo such as pharmaceuticals, toys, electronics, avionics, scientific equipment may require more sophisticated equipment and process changes whereas lower rated commodities would do well with basic upgrades.

2. **"Trouble tradelanes"** that are headaches due to drugs, human smuggling, theft, terrorist threat, piracy or counterfeit replacements of legitimate products. Certain regions of the world are conducive to recurring problems due to economic, cultural, religious or geo-political factors.

3. **The need to be predictive of problems** or issues before they begin and then to pre-emptively avoid them. Such as strikes, social unrest, weather, problems with personnel, logistical infrastructure weaknesses, etc. that would affect performance of the supply chain.

So, having identified the areas of pain, let's consider what can be done to alleviate them?

Potential Pinkerton Solution set:

1. Create a business development unit of "virtual experts" that would be able to plan, design, and implement a total holistic approach to security issues: personnel, process, technology, and physical. While technology would be utilized, it will still be personnel and processes that will be the keys to a successful solution set.

2. Identify high margin industries and tie security with ROI as a value proposition for these industries/companies. Example: re-deploy Pinkerton's current PDMA (Prescription Drug Marketing Act) Compliance practice to be more pre-emptive in nature via better processes and technologies to prevent tampering and counterfeiting in the pharma world.

3. Concentrate on end to end solution for the "trouble tradelanes" or regions of greatest concerns for companies. The emphasis is not to "bulletproof" a tradelane but to make the client's tradelane dramatically harder to infiltrate; that criminal and terrorist elements would shift their efforts elsewhere.

So what distinguishes Pinkerton/Securitas from the slew of consultancies, integrators, and various security firms that offer a solution set to the private and government sector clients?

Distinct Pinkerton Advantages:

1. **The reputation of Pinkerton** and its history will create positive image of what can be done to improve security plus the 21st century capabilities as mentioned above in Pinkerton Solution Set would make people realize that Pinkerton means business.

2. **The global presence of Securitas** is very important for global, multi-sourcing, and multi-layered networks of modern corporations and their joint venture partners and vendors. Having in-country representation and presence is crucial to create a level of credibility and also of "reach"

3. **The agility of size** (not as big as the "beltway" integrators with high ROI thresholds) and corporate coherence (compared to consultancies that are long on "tech" thinking but short on practical security applications).

Summary:

Pinkerton can and should take the initiative to build a Supply Chain Business Development Unit that would tap into these large market needs. If so then I would like to lead it to create an effective revenue generation tool.

My background in supply chain (planning, pricing, design, and execution), business development, industry knowledge, and creating leading edge security supply chain initiatives make me uniquely qualified for taking on this task.

Given the right resources, Pinkerton could forge an irresistible message and create a real market niche in the supply chain world.

EXHIBIT 1 (CONT'D)

John Lee's Position Papers:
Version 3: Pinkerton   Value Proposition

Cross selling (Leveraging)

Cross or matrix selling – the ability to leverage the existing base of customers by the following steps:

1st – combining and analyzing database of Pinkerton services utilized, markets served, market or firm intelligence sharing

2nd – map out areas of growth or better penetration with emphasis on upselling and/or selling across company lines
(example: guard services, cash handling, access control, alarm systems)

3rd - executing sales effort on targeted customers with various Pinkerton business units.

4th - advertising (internally) the success stories of this approach to increase acceptance and follow up on all viable leads.

Supply Chain Solutions (Beyond CTPAT and OSC)

Building off of the great work already done with CTPAT and OSC, help to create a coherent message of supply chain security, accountability and integrity. How?

Target high value products/industries such as: Pharmaceuticals, Tobacco, Liquor, Toys, Medical instrumentation, cosmetics and high fashion apparel. Relationships already exist such as Company X that could be strengthened and deepened.

Present solutions that encompass core competencies of Pinkerton such as: guard services, access controls, physical security, process security assessments, etc.

Possibly, present solutions that are easy segues into other profitable areas of security such as: RFID tagging, biometrics, etc.

Bottomline for the corporate customer: making sense of all the supply chain possibilities, choosing the right one for them, and executing these measures for them so that they can concentrate on their core competency (which is not security, obviously).

EXHIBIT 1 (CONT'D)

Value Proposition

International (true end to end solutions)

Doing all of the above will necessitate a truly global solution and Pinkerton/Securitas has the global reach to do a true womb-to-tomb approach of its security applications.

What can be done to be more effective?:

- Strengthen INTERNAL international relationships so that when a global project up for bid (or nonbid) is before us that there is true synchronization of all the disparate global branches and personnel in pushing for win and, when successful in winning bid, that the deployment is smoother (costing, design, pricing, implementation).

- Cull the opportunities that cross over borders. Example: XYZ is a large existing customer for Pinkerton in the US that has a very large presence in China and other nations. Look into what can be done on cross border initiatives such as: pulling all the services under a larger umbrella to have a team specifically tasked to handle XYZ and its needs worldwide (this would make their exposure to Securitas more seamless).

- Create on-demand, ad hoc global teams that will help to work on government or private/public sector initiatives or events which are usually very big in scope.
  Example: Port security upgrades, drug/product counterfeiting (brand protection), China Olympics, US Customs "green lane" initiative.

Legacy of security (not re-invention)

It is somewhat funny to see companies such as: Company X, XYZ Corp, and YYYZ, Inc., etc. re-casting themselves as security providers (in one sense or another). Securitas occupies a very unique space in that it has always been a security-based company especially with the former Burns and Pinkerton firms under its aegis.

Companies are struggling to make sense of the myriad of solutions and solutions providers that are out plying their wares. These customers are looking for a firm that will take them by the hand to develop a security plan that makes sense and then to execute with minimal issues.

I believe that Pinkerton/Securitas has the wherewithal to do the aforementioned tasks and to do it better than anyone in the marketplace. The true value proposition is simple: does anyone in the market offer the experiential depth, global breadth, and industry experience as Pinkerton/Securitas?

EXHIBIT 2

The Serious Job Finder's Schedule - Darren's version (Chapter 5)

Week 1

	Monday	Tuesday	Wednesday	Thursday	Friday
8:00 - 9:00 am	Research Company 1	Research Company 4	Research Company 7	Research Position Paper	Call Company 1,2,3,4
9:00 - 10:00 am	Research Company 1	Make Folder for Co. 4	Make Folder for Co. 7	Research Position Paper	Research Company 9
10:00 - 11:00 am	Make Folder for Co. 1	Call Company 1 and 2	Call Company 1,2, 3	Research Position Paper	Make Folder for Co. 9
11:00 - 12:00 pm	Research Company 2	Research Company 5	Break - goof off	Write Position Paper	Write Position Paper
12:00 - 1:00 pm	Lunch	Lunch	Lunch	Lunch	Lunch
1:00 - 2:00 pm	Research Company 2	Make Folder for Co. 5	Research Company 8	Write Position Paper	Write Position Paper
2:00 - 3:00 pm	Make Folder for Co. 2	Call Company 1,2, and 3	Make Folder for Co. 8	Write Position Paper	Research Company 10
3:00 - 4:00 pm	Take a break	Research Company 6	Follow up calls	Write Position Paper	Make Folder for Co. 10
4:00 - 5:00 pm	Research Company 3	Make Folder for Co. 6	Research Position Paper	Write Position Paper	Knock off early
5:00 - 6:00 pm	Make Folder for Co. 3	Finish Up	Finish Up	Finish Up	Done

Week 2

	Monday	Tuesday	Wednesday	Thursday	Friday
8:00 - 9:00 am	Research Company 11	Get ready for appt.	Mail off Position Papers	Research more information on industries	Get ready for appt
9:00 - 10:00 am	Make Folder for Co. 11	Attend appointment	Call company 2,3,4,5	Research more information on industries	Get ready for appt
10:00 - 11:00 am	Call Company 2,3,4	Post mortem on appt	Make notes in folders	Research more information on industries	Attend appointment
11:00 - 12:00 pm	Research Company 12	Send Thank you note to appointment	Meet with business person	Research more information on industries	Post mortem on appt
12:00 - 1:00 pm	Lunch	Lunch	Lunch with business person	Lunch	Lunch
1:00 - 2:00 pm	Make Folder for Co. 12	Finish Position Paper	Break - talk to people that are fun	Call company 3,4,5	Send Thank you note to appointment
2:00 - 3:00 pm	Call Company 2,3,4	Finish Position Paper	Break - talk to people that are fun	Refine your system	Research Company 13
3:00 - 4:00 pm	Finish Position Paper	Finish Position Paper	Have fun	Think about other avenues or people to call	Make Folder for Co. 13
4:00 - 5:00 pm	Finish Position Paper	Finish Position Paper	Have fun	Think about other avenues or people to call	Knock off
5:00 - 6:00 pm					

EXHIBIT 3

Darren's Position Paper: Version 3 (Chapter 5)

Landscape Overview and Suggestions

For the Gaming Industry

© 2007

EXHIBIT 3 (CONT'D)

Introduction

This report examines many factors affecting Microsoft Xbox 360's business from the point of view of an avid fan of the systems who also is interested in the strategic marketing of the product.

Strategic Suggestions

Acquire more Studios and Exclusive Titles

Halo 3 broke sales records by selling over 3 million copies in the span of two weeks. This is easily Microsoft's most important title and will likely sell millions of more 360s now and through this holiday season. The main question is *exactly* how many additional 360s will be sold on account of *Halo 3* and the highly anticipated *Mass Effect*. Analyst Mat Matthews of *Next Generation* states that *Halo 3* resulted in moving 150,000-200,000 systems in the month of September.[1] This number was derived by subtracting the sales rate of August from the sales rate of September. I believe many consumers who purchased 360s in August were motivated by the looming *Halo 3* launch in conjunction with the price cut. I expect sales of *Halo 3* and the Xbox 360 SKUs to remain strong through the holiday season.

However, I feel Microsoft does not have many big selling exclusive titles besides *Halo Wars* for 2008. My feelings are compounded by the fact that Microsoft has lost studios which used to produce blockbuster games exclusively for Xbox 360. The departure of Bungie (*Halo* series), EA's acquisition of BioWare/Pandemic (*Mass Effect, Jade Empire*), and Activision's acquisition of Bizarre Creations (*Project Gotham Racing* series) indicate a troubling trend for Microsoft since it is highly unlikely these studios will release exclusive titles for Microsoft without extremely lucrative (and costly) exclusivity contract signing.

Microsoft owns 7 studios that produce games for the 360, less than half the number of studios owned by Sony. This means that Sony has the capabilities to produce a lot more exclusive first-party titles than Microsoft is able to. To combat this, I suggest Microsoft acquire or sign exclusive deals with other studios to increase their software portfolio in the upcoming years. Helping to finance quality products such as *Gears of War* in exchange for exclusivity or buying financially hurting but talented studios like Lionhead (*Fable*) are great tactics that must be repeated. There are very few third party exclusives to go around due to rapid third-party publisher acquisitions and soaring development costs for the 360 and PS3 platforms. Microsoft should try to use its greater market share and less costly development cycle compared to Sony as a strong selling point in persuading third parties to develop exclusively on its platform.

---

[1] http://www.next-gen.biz/index.php?option=com_content&task=view&id=7648&Itemid=2&limit=1&limitstart=1

EXHIBIT 3 (CONT'D)

What will ultimately determine the winner in the upcoming years of the console war is exclusive content, primarily first-party content. From this perspective, I am skeptical of the Xbox 360 long-term sustainability. Microsoft must first and foremost secure exclusive hot titles, whether it be through acquisitions or exclusivity contract signing, if they wish to continue expanding market share and profits.

Strengthen Relationships with Third Party Vendors by Capitalizing on PS3's Development Difficulties

Developing games for the PS3 is notoriously difficult due to its complex system architecture. *Unreal Tournament 3,* a title which Sony paid big bucks to secure an earlier release over the 360 version, has been delayed due to development complications.[2] Furthermore, development difficulty often causes PS3 versions of multiplatform titles to be of inferior quality compared to Xbox 360 and PC versions (PS3 version of Vivendi Games's *F.E.A.R.* suffered from inferior graphics and stuttering frame rate while EA's *Madden NFL '08* ran at 30 frames-per-seconds compared to Xbox 360's 60 fps).

These inferior versions affect sales (360 version of Madden sold 896,600 copies in compared to PS3's 336,200).[3] This is a huge advantage for Microsoft to capitalize on since the only action Sony can counter with is to offer better customer service to third-party studios. Microsoft should emphasize the higher sales figures, lower cost, better quality, and decreased development complexity and frustration to persuade third party vendors to develop games for the Xbox 360 instead.

Diversify into Family Market without Diluting Brand Image among Hardcore Gamers

It appears as Microsoft is attempting to penetrate the casual, children, and family markets with the release of *Xbox Live Arcade, Viva Piñata,* and the upcoming *Scene It?: Lights, Camera, Action, Viva Piñata: Party Animals* and *Banjo Kazooie 3* titles. Although expanding market share through diversification is a great long-term goal, this should prove to be a challenge due to consumer perceptions of the Xbox as a brand that caters to young males in their teens and early twenties.

To expand beyond this brand image without alienating hardcore gamers, Microsoft should consider attempting to gain exclusivity on **established** IP that appeals to young gamers and hardcore gamers alike. Examples of this concept executed effectively include the *Kingdom Hearts* series for the PS2 and the *Super Smash Bros.* and *Mario Kart* series for Nintendo. The *Kingdom Hearts* games combined Disney IP (which appeals to children as well as older Disney fans) and Square Enix's *Final Fantasy* IP (which appeals to the hardcore gamer). The *Super Smash Bros.* and *Mario Kart* series feature easy pick-up-and-play mechanics fused with an appropriate level of complexity that appeals to multiple market segments.

---

[2] http://www.gamespot.com/ps3/action/unrealtournament2007/news.html?sid=6180254&om_act=convert&om_clk=newsfeatures&tag=newsfeatures;title;1
[3] http://www.shacknews.com/onearticle.x/48959

EXHIBIT 3 (CONT'D)

The above examples dealt with established IP applied to innovative and fun gameplay concepts. Established IP such as Disney and Mario in itself appeals to multiple demographics. Microsoft should approach companies with alluring IP (Disney, Warner Bros., Marvel, etc.) in attempt to subsidize mass-appeal products in exchange for exclusivity.

Protect Image of Xbox Live Offering the Best Online Experience

Microsoft currently enjoys a huge lead over Sony and Nintendo in offering an easy-to-use and enjoyable online interface and experience. While the competition is offering free online, Microsoft can very well continue charging subscription fees without losing too many customers as long as they offer the best service and best online games. Nintendo's and Sony's relative online inexperience will most likely contribute to numerous glitches, lagging issues, cheaters, and connectivity errors Microsoft should exploit.

A small yet important advantage Xbox Live (XBL) should exploit against Playstation Network (PSN) is the Universal Friends List (as proof of being more user-friendly, time efficient, and customer-centric). XBL offers one universal list that allows players to see what games ALL of their online friends are playing and allows easy messaging and joining of friends' games. PSN lacks this function. Instead, PSN users must select a game they wish to play and then see whether any of their friends are currently playing the same game. Furthermore, PSN currently does not allow gamers to send or receiving mid-game messages or game invites, making it more difficult for online friends to interact and play together.

Counter PSN Multimedia Expansion

In an interview with *Financial Times*, Sony chief executive Sir Howard Stringer briefly mentioned plans for PSN to carry music and video downloads, possibly in early 2008.[4]

Details of PSN's multimedia plans are unknown. Will they provide a service similar to iTunes and sell music files, movies, and TV shows? It seems likely. Incorporating the catalogs of Sony Pictures and Sony Music would be a great potential move to support this business strategy.

I would advise Microsoft to consider expanding their multimedia services to counter this move. Some changes to consider:

- In addition to "renting" movies, Microsoft could grant users the option to pay a little more to purchase movies that remain on the users hard drive.

---

[4] http://www.ft.com/cms/s/0/f039c15c-7b81-11dc-8c53-0000779fd2ac.html

EXHIBIT 3 (CONT'D)

- Incorporate Zune Marketplace with XBL to counter Sony's music offering. This will give XBL quick access to a music service provider while also likely boost the awareness and popularity of Zune and XBL.
- Eventual Removal of Microsoft Points in favor of real currency. PSN and iTunes list real currencies rather than points as Microsoft and Nintendo does. Microsoft Points makes it harder and less user-friendly for consumers to determine how much items cost in Zune Marketplace and XBL Marketplace. While a point-system avoids the complications of listing numerous currencies and may induce more impulse purchases (since some consumers may view their points as "play money" and cease associating the points with their true monetary value), I feel they should eventually be replaced since doing makes the Zune Marketplace and the XBL Marketplace a more user-friendly experience which could increase sales. With the competition from iTunes and Sony, I feel Microsoft needs to do everything they can to offer consumers the best possible online user experience.

Product Bundling

To counter hot, potentially system-selling PS3 titles such as *Metal Gear Solid 4* and *Final Fantasy XIII,* Microsoft should consider announcing a great product bundle leading up to the release dates of these PS3 titles. Bundling a Xbox 360 with a great game (or two) like *Halo 3* will likely take attention away from PS3 and induce consumers to purchase a 360 instead.

Counter Image of Faulty Hardware Provider

Due to the widespread awareness and coverage on national news regarding Xbox 360s hardware problems such as the "red ring of death," I would highly advise Microsoft to aggressively spread a message of offering reliable and durable 360s **if** the "Falcon" and "Jasper" 360 models resolve the Xbox 360's technical problems.

The Xbox 360 brand image has been greatly damaged to the widely known hardware problems, which greatly increases consumers' perceived risk of purchase. While the 3-year warranty extension is a good short-term move, I feel it is inadequate in terms of inducing purchase among many consumers. When I have conversed with Xbox 360 owners who experienced hardware failure both in person and online, many expressed their annoyance of having to wait for their systems to be repaired or replaced. I believe the perceived fear of having a Xbox 360 fail despite the 3-year warranty represents a high barrier for the Xbox 360 in obtaining greater market share.

I suggest Microsoft must aggressively investigate solutions to this problem via new product models. Once Microsoft feels confident in a new product model through vigorous QA testing, they should aggressively communicate this message

EXHIBIT 3 (CONT'D)

to the media and press in order to reverse consumers' negative perceptions and induce purchase.

Allow Studios Greater Creative Freedom

When asked about *Halo* series game developer Bungie Studios' split from Microsoft, Bungie Franchise and Community Leader Brian Allard said:

> … it was something that we had to do as a group to creatively continue to expand and continue what we want to do. As [Bungie's Jason Jones] so aptly put it, we're a shark that just has to keep moving to stay alive, otherwise we felt that we'd start to stagnate and potentially lose interest, and maybe even lose some of our teams.[5]

Later in the interview, Allard reveals that Bungie started thinking about splitting after the release of *Halo 2*.[6] While the details of the split are unknown due to confidentiality agreements, the interview seems to infer Bungie's dissatisfaction with the amount of creative freedom granted by Microsoft as well as disinterest in working with the same *Halo* IP indefinitely. Assuming this is true; Microsoft should allow highly talented studios more freedom to explore new ideas and game concepts. Instead of forcing a studio to make a sequel, it is often better to hand over the existing IP to another studio who is capable and willing to make a quality sequel to a hit game. Microsoft handed the *Halo* IP to Ensemble Studios to develop *Halo Wars*, a good strategic move Microsoft should repeat to avoid in-house developer burnout.

Maintain a Presence in Japan

Although Microsoft has not been successful in Japan, it is important to still maintain a market presence there. The reason is that by doing so, Microsoft can potentially build stronger relationships with Japanese publishers who desire to release more titles catered to Western tastes (as North America represents the largest and fast-growing market for video games). Companies like Square Enix has publicly declared their intentions of a more global strategy,[7] which means they plan on selling more games to North America and Europe. Japan is home to many great companies such as Capcom, Konami, Square Enix, Namco, and Tecmo whose products do very well in international markets. Many of these companies who use to release games exclusively on Playstation in the last console generation are now releasing games both on Xbox 360 and PS3, thus taking competitive advantage away from Sony. This outcome is partly due to Microsoft's continued presence in Japan despite disappointing sales in the country.

---

[5] http://www.next-gen.biz/index.php?option=com_content&task=view&id=7416&Itemid=2
[6] http://www.next-gen.biz/index.php?option=com_content&task=view&id=7416&Itemid=2&limit=1&limitstart=1
[7] http://www.computerandvideogames.com/article.php?id=172838

EXHIBIT 3 (CONT'D)

If a talented Japanese studio is hurting financially, Microsoft should consider helping them in exchange for exclusivity. Sony aided Square (now Square Enix) after the firm failed with the expensive *Final Fantasy: Spirits Within* film.[8] Square Enix has been producing blockbuster *Final Fantasy* titles exclusively for Sony platforms ever since. Microsoft should mimic a similar tactic when appropriate.

Conclusion

With the rising development costs of videogame and rapid consolidation of studios, it will become harder than ever to acquire exclusive content. Microsoft should investigate acquiring talented studios or subsidizing their projects in exchange for exclusivity.

Due to the Playstation 3's architecture, it can be very challenging and costly for studios to develop games for. Microsoft should emphasize the Xbox 360's higher sales figures, lower cost, better quality, and decreased development complexity and frustration to persuade third party vendors to develop games for the Xbox 360.

To appeal to the casual, children, and family markets without alienating hardcore gamers, Microsoft attempt to gain exclusivity on titles that feature gameplay and established IP that appeals to young gamers and hardcore gamers alike.

Microsoft must protect their brand image as offering the best online service and experience. Doing so involves continuing to expand useful features to counter Sony's multimedia moves and exploit Nintendo's and Sony's shortcomings and inexperience as providers of online game play.

To counter a potentially system-selling release from Nintendo or Sony, Microsoft could counter with a great product bundling.

Microsoft should rigorously investigate new product models for a design that can fixes the technical problems such as the "red ring of death." Once this model passes rigorous QA testing, Microsoft should aggressively advertise and promote this new model to reduce consumer's perceived risk of purchase.

To maintain innovative and high quality products while reducing studio burnout, Microsoft should grant highly talented studios the freedom to explore new game concepts and ideas.

Despite facing losses in Japan, Microsoft should still maintain a presence in the region to strengthen ties and relationships with Japanese developers who can make games that appeal to Western gamers.

---

[8] http://www.ffonline.com/news/news.php?article=2001-10-09

EXHIBIT 4

The Serious Job Finder's Schedule - Blanks w/notes (Chapter 7)
Following 6 pages

WEEK 1

	Monday	Tuesday	Wednesday	Thursday	Friday
8:00 - 9:00 am					
9:00 - 10:00 am					
10:00 - 11:00 am					
11:00 - 12:00 pm					
12:00 - 1:00 pm	Lunch				
1:00 - 2:00 pm		Lunch			
2:00 - 3:00 pm			Lunch		
3:00 - 4:00 pm				Lunch	
4:00 - 5:00 pm					Lunch
5:00 - 6:00 pm					

Things to have done by end of the week:

- ☒ Get materials in place to carry out your upcoming tasks
- ☒ Have a "work week" schedule that you have begun to start the process
- ☒ Think about 1 - 2 target industries
- ☒ Have list of possible 16 firms that you would be interested in the 1 or 2 target industries

WEEK 2

	Monday	Tuesday	Wednesday	Thursday	Friday
8:00 - 9:00 am					
9:00 - 10:00 am					
10:00 - 11:00 am					
11:00 - 12:00 pm					
12:00 - 1:00 pm	Lunch				
1:00 - 2:00 pm		Lunch			
2:00 - 3:00 pm			Lunch		
3:00 - 4:00 pm				Lunch	
4:00 - 5:00 pm					Lunch
5:00 - 6:00 pm					

Things to have done by end of the week:

☒ Identified viable 1 or 2 industry(ies) that you plan to work in

☒ Identified and researched possible associations that you will be joining to leverage

☒ Written a rough draft of position paper (2-3 pages maximum)

WEEK 3

	Monday	Tuesday	Wednesday	Thursday	Friday
8:00 - 9:00 am					
9:00 - 10:00 am					
10:00 - 11:00 am					
11:00 - 12:00 pm					
12:00 - 1:00 pm	Lunch				
1:00 - 2:00 pm		Lunch			
2:00 - 3:00 pm			Lunch		
3:00 - 4:00 pm				Lunch	
4:00 - 5:00 pm					Lunch
5:00 - 6:00 pm					

Things to have done by end of the week:

☒ Finish the research and pick the Top 4 firms with information folders on 16 firms total

☒ Create folder for each targeted firm with information sheets: conversation log, general information and organizational chart

☒ Decide which associations to join based on research of Week 2 – don't go broke in the process. If the fees to join are in $100 - $200 range (or less) then it should be fine. Consider this an investment in your future!

WEEK 4

	Monday	Tuesday	Wednesday	Thursday	Friday
8:00 - 9:00 am					
9:00 - 10:00 am					
10:00 - 11:00 am					
11:00 - 12:00 pm					
12:00 - 1:00 pm	Lunch	Lunch	Lunch	Lunch	Lunch
1:00 - 2:00 pm					
2:00 - 3:00 pm					
3:00 - 4:00 pm					
4:00 - 5:00 pm					
5:00 - 6:00 pm					

Things to have done by end of the week:

☒ Understand Fearless Method technique and practice it with a friend or family member

☒ Research best numbers to use to contact CEO or department head

☒ Call the numbers to get to targeted person in target company

☒ Chase down all targeted companies and pursue till you have definitely hit dead end – no progress, simply blocked, no call backs or emails, no invitation to move forward, etc.

WEEK 5

	Monday	Tuesday	Wednesday	Thursday	Friday
8:00 - 9:00 am					
9:00 - 10:00 am					
10:00 - 11:00 am					
11:00 - 12:00 pm					
12:00 - 1:00 pm	Lunch				
1:00 - 2:00 pm		Lunch			
2:00 - 3:00 pm			Lunch		
3:00 - 4:00 pm				Lunch	
4:00 - 5:00 pm					Lunch
5:00 - 6:00 pm					

Things to have done by end of the week:

- ☒ Make more calls to get to decisionmakers from the Top 4 target list.

- ☒ Make calls to Mid 4 target list as Top 4 targets are eliminated either by total rejection or getting a strong lead on the decision makers

- ☒ Attend association meetings and push for getting on a board or committee

WEEK 6

	Monday	Tuesday	Wednesday	Thursday	Friday
8:00 - 9:00 am					
9:00 - 10:00 am					
10:00 - 11:00 am					
11:00 - 12:00 pm					
12:00 - 1:00 pm	Lunch	Lunch	Lunch	Lunch	Lunch
1:00 - 2:00 pm					
2:00 - 3:00 pm					
3:00 - 4:00 pm					
4:00 - 5:00 pm					
5:00 - 6:00 pm					

Things to have done by end of the week:

- ☒ Continue to approach and process the Top 4, Mid 4, Low 4 targets
- ☒ Set up meetings for informational interviews about the topic you wrote the position paper about
- ☒ Go to meetings of targeted associations and work to get on a board or committee

EXHIBIT 5

Conversation Log Sheet - Sample (Chapter 9)

Conversation Log Sheet
Company: Monolithic Corp

Date: 6/11/13
Time: 3:05 pm

Person's Name/Title: Helen Roper – Project Director
Phone/Email: 253 – 698 8954

Topic: Possible times to meet – Helen said next week looks good – 6/18 Tues at 3 pm her office

Follow Up Action: Need to finish my position paper to get ready!

Date: 6/19/13
Time: 11:00 am

Person's Name/Title: Terry, asst to James Emerson
Phone/Email: 206 567 8909

Topic: Meeting to get together post interview/meeting with Helen Roper

Follow Up Action: Meeting with Jim Emerson, Project Manager at Starbucks on 6th and Seneca for ½ hr to discuss position paper and possible job posting (per Helen Roper) at the Special Materials division under J. Emerson

---

Date: 7/2/13
Time: 2:12 pm

Person's Name/Title: Jeff Natt, Project Lead reporting to Jim Emerson
Phone/Email: 253 698 8957

Topic: Not able to meet due to 4th of July break

Follow Up Action: After 7/9 Tuesday then call him to set up possible job interview for unposted position!

EXHIBIT 5 (CONT'D)

Conversation Log Sheet - Blank (Chapter 5)

Conversation Log Sheet
Company: _____

Date:_____
Time:_____

Person's Name/Title:_____
Phone/Email: _____

Topic:_____

Follow Up Action: _____

....

Date:_____
Time:_____

Person's Name/Title:_____
Phone/Email: _____

Topic:_____

Follow Up Action: _____

....

Date:_____
Time:_____

Person's Name/Title:_____
Phone/Email: _____

Topic:_____

Follow Up Action: _____

EXHIBIT 6

General Information Sheet - Sample (Chapter 9)

General Information Sheet

Company: Monolithic Corp
Industry: Plastics and Extrusions/Moldings

HQ Address: 4560 Fleet Street, Renton, Washington 98056

Main Phone: 253 698 8000

Website: www.MonolithicCorp.com
www.Monolithicplastics.com
Parent Corp: www.Powerplastics.com

Last year's Revenues: $45 million
Last year's Profits or Operating Income: $5.3 million

How Big?: Regional – Washington, Oregon, Idaho, Utah and Northern Calif
Distribution centers in Kent and Renton, Washington and Tigard, OR

Products: Snap-eze plastic products (building materials, industrial, retail and scientific), PVC pipe layer, "special materials" – amalgams?

People/ Phone/Emails:

Gennifer Lewis VP – 253 698 8933 glewis@monolithiccorp.com
    Guy Tennant – Gennifer's admin 253 698 8944

Helen Roper Project Director - 253 698 8955 – hroper@monolithiccorp.com
NOTE: Helen reports to Gennifer

Jim Emerson Project Manager – 253 698 8512 jemerson1@monolithiccorp.com
NOTE: Jim reports to Helen
    Terry Whitfield – Jim's admin 206 567 8909 (Seattle mobile)

Jeff Natt, Project Lead (reporting to Jim Emerson)
Phone/Email: 253 698 8957 jnatt@monolithiccorp.com or jeff.natt134@gmail.com

EXHIBIT 6

General Information Sheet - Blank (Chapter 9)

General Information Sheet

Company: _____

Industry: _____

HQ Address: _____
_____

Main Phone: _____

Website: _____

Parent Corporation?
_____
_____

Last year's Revenues: _____
Last year's Profits or Operating Income: _____

How Big?: _____

Products: _____
_____

People/ Phone/Emails: _____
_____
_____
_____
_____

Notes: _____
_____
_____
_____
_____
_____

Call Scripts (Chapter 10)

IMPORTANT NOTE: Before making these calls you should know the company's CEO name and the next level down (VP, EVP, SVP, COO, CFO) person's name.

Gatekeeper Call:
1. Main switchboard operator:

Branch 1:

Call the main number of the targeted company and you get an operator then:

"Hello, please connect me to (CEO's full name) office"

then he/she sends the call up to CEO's office – see CEO's administrative assistant script

Branch 1a:

You say the above but they ask you what this is all about. You say:

"This is about the (position paper's topic) and possible engagement with your company"

If the operator still asks questions or treats this as a sales call or gives you directions to send an email for general requests then politely thank them and hang up. See Branch 3 below-blocker mode.

Branch 3:

Try different number combinations of the last 4 digits of the main phone number and say to whoever picks up the line:

"Hi, I've been bounced around a bit. Could you please send me to (CEO's full name) office"

If you have tried this tactic 5 times and still no one is sending you through then STOP!! Proceed to Branch 4.

Branch 4:

Try the next level down executive – the one that manages the silo or function within the company that you are interested in – and call the main number with his/her name. Repeat process of Branch 1, 1a, 3 if you cannot get through. You will get through!

For mechanical operator see Playbook's Branch 2, 2a tactic!

EXHIBIT 7 (CONT'D)

2. CEO's administrative assistant

You will probably talk to the CEO's administrative assistant. Say:

> "Hi, my name is (your first name) and I was wondering if you could guide me as to who is the head of (branch, function, division that you are interested in)?"

When asked what this is all about then say:

> "This is about the (position paper's topic) and possible engagement with your company"

He/she may give you information. If they do give the next level down executive name then ask the person for his/her FIRST name (such as Norma). Thank Norma and ask her what is a way to get a hold of that person, Norma may pass you to operator or connect you directly to that person's office or hang up and dial the general number again to ask for that next level down executive by name.

If the CEO administrative assistant is not sure who it is you are seeking then say:

> "Could it be (name of next level down executive)?"

Then ask for her first name (Norma) and thank and hang up.

IMPORTANT NOTE: you must get the CEO's assistant's name! Example: Norma the assistant. This is very important!

3. Next level down executive's administrative assistant:

Call and tell the executive's assistant :

> "Hi, my name is (your full name) and I would like to speak to (executive's name next level down). I was referred to him/her by Mr. CEO's assistant (Norma in this example)."

If he/she asks you the nature of the call then you tell him/her that it pertains to (position paper's topic).

At this point there are two routes this can take:

A. The executive's admin takes a message or sends you to voicemail then:

Voicemail: Leave a short message that has this to say:

> "Hi (executive's first name), my name is (your full name) and I was referred to you by Norma, the administrative assistant of (CEO's name). Could you please call me at (your mobile number). Thank you."

IMPORTANT NOTE: That is it! DO NOT say anything more or give explanations of the nature of the call

Helping Hint:

If there is no call back then give it approx. 3 hours then call back and leave another message. You are done for that call for that day.

EXHIBIT 7 (CONT'D)

B. The admin refuses to let you talk to her boss then ask them who should you talk to. Get this person's name, title and phone number. Call this referred to person

> ✓ Rehearse this series of blockades with a family/friend with you going over the lines so that it trips off your tongue more naturally!
>
> **Reality CHECK**

Actionable Person Call:

1. Next level down from CEO (VP, SVP, EVP, COO, CFO, Head of Legal or HR, etc):

You get the executive on the line. Take a deep breath, smile and do the following:

a. Introduce yourself

b. State that you were referred to him by CEO's admin (Norma in this case)

**IMPORTANT NOTE: You must give out the CEO's admin's first name –
this is information that you cannot look up or make up – it legitimizes your call!!**

c. State that you were calling to find out more information about his/her company's participation in the (position paper's topic) and beginning a dialogue on this topic and was wondering if he/she was the person to talk to. Then shut up.

If he/she then asks why you are interested in it then say that you are thinking about engaging with the company on a fulltime or consulting basis on such a project.

Helping Hint:
Take quick, bulletized notes of what he/she is saying to you – you will need them later!

d. If the executive says you should talk to HR or personnel then say that you did a position paper on the topic and really would like someone like him/her to see if this was the kind of work that the company was doing

e. Ask for meeting with him/her **OR** someone that they feel would be good to talk about the topic. Keep quiet. Take notes as to where or what he/she wants you to go. If he/she tells you the director or manager who is responsible then ask him how you can get a hold of him – write down name, title, and phone/email information of his/her subordinate

f. Thank him/her (you may get a chance to talk to him later)

EXHIBIT 7 (CONT'D)

2. Second level down (director, AVP, senior manager):

Call the manager or director that was referenced or recommended by the VP and tell him/her what the VP said and that you are trying to achieve a better understanding of the company and its work in (position paper topic)

Ask for a face to face meeting – pick a date next week and let him/her guide you as to when it would be best to meet.

Rules of Engagement:

Hold yourself accountable to make two calls a day

Emphasis on getting a face to face meeting so that you will be able to find out more about the company and its work in (position paper topic)

✓ **Reality CHECK**

It is most probably at this level (one level down from the VP or department head) that the hiring authority resides for 70% of the jobs out there. Unless it is a hiring by selection committee, then you will be talking to only one of the hiring managers which is good if he/she becomes your Personal Champion to the others!

EXHIBIT 8

Call Progress Tree (Chapter 10)

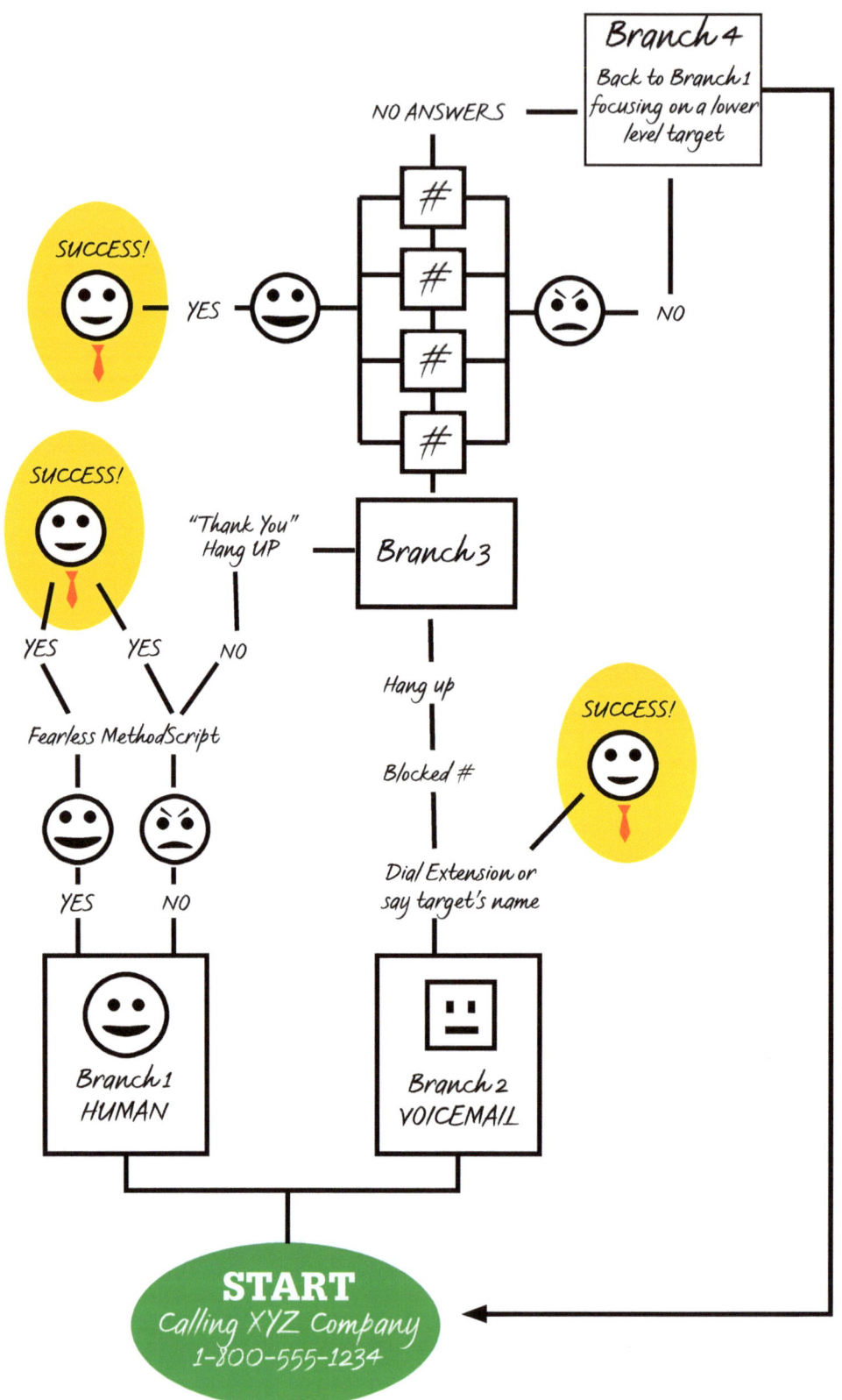

EXHIBIT 9
Template Baseline Questions (Chapter 12)

- ☐ Company/Division/Dept?
- ☐ Contact person's name/title/location/contact information (office, mobile, fax, email)?
- ☐ The overall growth of the company? What markets does it occupy? Where are areas of growth?
- ☐ What are you in charge of? What is the geographical footprint?
- ☐ What are some of the initiatives that the company is working on in the (position paper topic)?
- ☐ Where are the areas for growth when it comes to (position paper topic)?
- ☐ Are there any downsides or pitfalls when it comes to (position paper topic)?
- ☐ How did the (position paper topic) become so important or relevant and when did it really catch fire?
- ☐ How can this (position paper topic) change the industry or company for better?
- ☐ How can this (position paper topic) make it worse for the industry or company?
- ☐ What are things this company is doing to be the leader (or ahead of the pack) when it comes to the (position paper topic)?
- ☐ Where are there readings (trade journal, books, or websites) that I might learn more about (position paper topic)?
- ☐ Where are there areas of opportunity that someone like me could look to if I wanted to pursue (position paper topic) with the company?
- ☐ How does one get started to be considered for either contract or fulltime work on such a project?
- ☐ Who could I talk to regarding this topic more than what we've covered?

LAST POINT – BUT VERY IMPORTANT:

- ☐ I would like to refine my position paper but was wondering if you could read it and critique it?
- ☐ NOW is the time to give him the position paper – with statement that you will check back with him/her in about a week to hear their thoughts. Please do what you say that you will!

Helping Hint:
It truly is okay to have this list of questions on your lap to read out and to write down the response like you did in college classes. IT IS NOT RUDE, on the contrary, it is very complimentary that you are paying that much attention but keep eye contact whenever possible!

EXHIBIT 10
Recommended Reading List

✓ ***Propel: Five Ways to Amp-Up Your Marketing and Accelerate Business**
by Whitney Keyes.
Published by The Career Press Inc.*

This book helps you visualize what to do for marketing a product to strategize and focus on what is important. The applicability here is that when you think of branding and brand management – think of the product as YOU!

✓ ***Selling to VITO the Very Important Top Officer: Get to the Top. Get to the Point. Get to the Sale**
by Anthony Parinello.
Published by Adams Business (Adams Media)*

This book was very helpful when I needed to punch through the barricades by simply avoiding them! It has a helicopter effect by taking you to the top and going to the appropriate level.

✓ ***SPIN Selling**
by Neil Rackham
Published by McGraw Hill, Inc.*

A very powerful way to engage with a "buyer" by looking at what is important to him/her. This trains you to think of what an employer (buyer) thinks/feels is important and to address the message accordingly.

www.ingramcontent.com/pod-product-compliance
Lightning Source LLC
Chambersburg PA
CBHW042023150426
43198CB00002B/46